Finding Happily...
No Rules, No Frogs
And, No Pretending

COLLETTE GEE

Finding Happily... No Rules, No Frogs, And No Pretending
Copyright © 2021 by Collette Gee

Less Is More Press LLC
First Publishing – 2021
Printed in the United States

ISBN (978-1-7330774-2-2)

Less Is More Press LLC
30 N. Gould Street, Ste. 10223
Sheridan, WY 82801
www.lessismorepress.com

Cover Design by:
Michael C. Gonzalez @
www.BDMcreative.com

DEDICATION

To my dear Aunt Kelly: I pray wherever you are, you found your happily . . .

"'Happily Ever After' is Not an Ending;
It is a journey."

—COLLETTE GEE

ACKNOWLEDGMENTS

I want to send a special thanks to the love of my life, my best friend, and my life partner Frank for his unwavering faith, love and support. Luckily for me, Frank and I met at a time in my life, when I was NOT following "The Rules," acting "like a Bitch," or pretending to be someone I was not. He has loved me unconditionally and for that I am so grateful.

I also thank him for creating **Less Is More Press LLC** publishing so that our families, friends and loved ones can have a creative platform to share their stories.

I also want to thank my best friend Tyson who supported me in more ways than one. From the moment I told Tyson I wanted to write this book he was the one friend who not only believed I would do it, but he stayed a true and loyal friend when all of my other friends fell by the wayside.

I want to thank Michael Gonzalez of **BDM Creative** for my wonderful book cover and website design.

I also want to thank my children and my mother. Without them I would not be the strong and loving woman I am today.

And last, but not least I want to give a shout out to my clients and all of my readers who like me continue to believe in love despite the challenges and heartaches. May each of you "Find Your Happily."

CONTENTS

Introduction

What little girl doesn't know that all too familiar fairy tale scenario; Once upon a time, in a faraway land filled with lush meadows, singing birds and burbling brooks, there lived a beautiful princess. A princess so beautiful and fair in fact, that the evil witch, ogre, or typical fairy tale bad guy is determined to have her locked away in a castle surrounded by moats, thick forests, and huge monsters.

That's where Prince Charming comes in!

This brave, valiant, dashing figure is determined to rescue the princess, with no regard for the danger it poses. He fearlessly climbs the mountain, sails the Seven Seas, fights the seven-headed serpent, slays the dragon, triumphs against the evil empire and rescues the princess, and the two of them mount his splendid stallion and gallop off to the prince's magnificent kingdom where everyone rejoices over the prince's safe return and welcomes the princess with open arms.

The story ends with a splendid wedding to end all weddings and the prince and the princess live happily ever after.

Or, do they?

These fairy tales of old (and some not so old) would have us believe that this is where the story ends. If we could only learn to stand up straight, learn the art of being demure, perfect our curtsy, sew, cook and sing like an angel, all the while perfecting our feminine wiles, we too can attract our Prince Charming and live happily ever after. All we would have to do is pretend, pretend, and pretend.

So... Exactly how do we accomplish this?

I examined many books on the market designed to teach women how to attract "Mr. Right." I researched lessons on how to make it past the first date, what to say and not to say, how to dress, and when and how to ration out the first kiss. Book after book were filled with instructions on how to be and how not to be.

The more I read and compared notes, the stronger my questions became:

When is it okay to stop pretending?
Do we ever get to just be ourselves?

Armed with the most popular how-to guides written by "relationship experts," I began my journey. Not just for myself, but for all women whose fate lies in finding the answers to the questions I pose.

If you are one of the lucky women out there who is just reading this book for entertainment, I would like to thank you. It is my sincere hope that you will continue reading and enjoying this book. However, if you are a woman like me and are reading this book because you are pressed to know the answers, I offer you my sentiments. I understand firsthand some of the frustrations you, along with many women like you, have experienced.

I cannot begin to tell you the countless times I have found myself sitting outdoors on a splendid afternoon, engaged in a conversation over lunch with some of my best girlfriends, swapping and sharing hopeless relationship stories. Stories, usually beginning something like:

"Okay ladies, I just do not know what to do. I went on my first date with the guy I met last week. We met at that cute little coffee place not too far from my house and we talked for almost two hours straight, sharing stories and laughing at one another's jokes. It was really nice.

The conversation really flowed, and the energy was really good. After we were done he walked me to my car, kissed me on the cheek and said how much he had enjoyed meeting and spending time with me and how he couldn't wait to see me again. Sigh... That was over two weeks ago and he hasn't called me, returned my calls, emailed or texted me!"

Sound familiar?

For many women, including me, this story is all too familiar. In fact, the entire scenario rings true. Yet another heartfelt "not-love" story. Always beginning with lots of hope and promise and ending with a feeling that looms over you like a dark cloud about to rain down on your parade. On such a miserable day, no friend (and not even on one of the most beautiful days of summer when you get to finally wear those Jimmy-Choo shoes) can make you feel better.

Yes, you've been there and may still be there. So you have no problem sympathizing with the poor woman whose just revealed the dagger sticking in her heart. Of course, she is expecting you, her closest friends, to pull it out and then use all of your skills and strategies to logically advise her what her next step should be to heal her wounded heart. She is expecting you to reach into your Louis Vuitton bags and pull out "the cure to end all failed relationships" advice.

And, what is this miraculous cure?
And, how far are we willing to go to find it?

Once you start looking for dating advice, it seems everyone has some to offer. Only after you have been the receiver of some of the worst advice from your family, friends, loved ones, the mailman, the butcher and the baker, do you finally reach the point where enough is enough. "I'm not going to listen to or take any more advice from anyone else," you declare, "unless he or she is an expert!"

Ah yes, the expert!

In nearly every bookstore, and likely hidden in some obscure location within, is the most dreaded section of the bookstore: the **SELF-HELP** section. And, despite the dreaded titles: *Have Him at Hello*, *Why Men Love Bitches* and *He's Just Not That Into You* (which are enough to make you gag) women venture in with the hope of finding some quick-fix-solution, written by an "expert" that not only promises to teach them, *How To Catch And Keep A Man,* but also how to "Live Happily Ever After."

In many ways the self-help section reminds me of the sordid feeling you might get walking down the aisle of a seedy adult bookstore. You go in, get out, and go home to get off --- hoping no one sees you.

Because I believe in supporting other fellow authors, I will admit that there are some good dating books out there that offer some solid and sound advice, and that may resonate deeply with you, and that you can even put into practice. However, the vast majority of dating books do not work, nor do they help women find the man of their dreams, because life is not pulled straight out of a storybook, and true love does not begin with the first kiss or even the first date, it begins and ends with SELF.

Now, I can already hear some of your arguments that this book sounds like another one of those "woo-woo" self-help books that promises *"Love Will Find You."* But, only after you learn how to *"Act Like A BITCH"* and *"Think Like a Man."*

However, the premise of this book is **NOT** to teach you how to out-manipulate men, play "hard to get," or pretend to play by "the rules" just to "hook a man." Instead, what you will find in these pages that follow is one message coming through loud and clear:

Happily Ever After is not An Ending; It's a Journey.

What To Expect

The pages that follow is a collection of short stories about me and several different people's dating and relationship challenges. In the end some of the stories end in happily ever after, some do not. Unlike fairy tales the stories in this book are real; only the names have been changed in order to protect people's identity.

The Objective?

Instead of the traditional dating guides (which is what most dating books inadvertently are) this book uses real life stories to show the lengths women will go through to find love and happiness.

Every woman can appreciate a good story, especially one with a happy ending. Right! After all, the best love stories entertain, inspire and allow us to use our imagination, thereby inserting ourselves into the story as one of the characters, thus exploring different outcomes and solutions in our own lives.

More traditional dating guides use outlines that provide the reader with a "how-to" manual (that usually does not work), to help them fix the problem: YOU. The problem with this approach is that relationships are not based off of a cookie-cutter format because each person is unique. However, through stories we can model, imitate and learn what works best for us. This is the way children learn and us adults are no different.

You can also think of this book in the same manner you watch or read a romantic story over and over again. You become so intrigued with the romantic subplot, that you begin to adopt the characters romantic experience as your own. Perhaps hoping the characters "happily ever after's" will rub off on you. This is known as a vicarious experience.

Vicarious experiences can be a great way for you to observe and model a new, or desired behavior. The reason why this model sometimes fails or goes wrong, (particularly in film) is because dating gurus and film executives that write and produce films, TV shows and books with romantic subplots, create a false sense of reality in order to cash in on your lonely heart. While they could create stories that depict the messy and sometimes complicated things that come along with dating and relationships (which is what you will find in this book), they serve you a fairy tale story from a Hollywood platform.

Lights, camera, action; The End!

If You Are Ready to Find YOUR Happily; Keep Reading!

If you are ready to rethink dating and relationships and find love under your own terms, then keep reading. If you are ready to stop doing "the rules," kissing magic frogs and pretending to be someone you are not, then keep reading.

This is the last dating and relationship book you will ever need!

No more books that suggest you play by "the rules" – i.e., no sex until the third or fourth date, never make him dinner, do not accept an invitation less than three days before, or do not ever call him, and so on. You will no longer need those books. Toss them!

Nor, will you ever have to watch another fairy tale ending that includes riding off into the sunset with a Disney soundtrack playing in the background.
No thanks, Disney!!!

Instead, as you read each of the stories in the chapters that follow you will learn that there is more than one path to find your happily, and while doing the rules, kissing magic frogs or pretending may work for some, what is important is what works best for you.

CHAPTER TWO

The Rescue Fantasy

**Your Attention Please:
No One Is Coming to Save You;
You Must Save Yourself**

No One Is Coming!

Many ears ago after I found myself in another failed relationship from a man I loved (and, who I believed loved me back) I cried for days on end over the breakup, praying and asking the universe, "Why?!!!"

Suddenly, I had an epiphany; I realized that I was operating under the assumption that it was my partners job to make me happy and that it was my job to make him happy. I gasped! Because, I realized that *my* joy and my happiness was hinged on *his* happiness. I wondered how this could be and why I continuously found myself so dependent on him (or other people) to feel good about my life. I knew it was time that I did something different, perhaps rethink relationships and my ideologies and thoughts about love.

I began my research first by reading several self-help books. Next, I attended workshops, trainings and seminars that all focused on healthy relationships. I listened to gurus like, Pat Allen and Matthew Hussey. I even watched movies like, *How to Lose a Guy In 10 Days, Hitch* and *Act Like a Lady.*

My hope was that I would find the solution to my relationship problems (or, at the very least) I would learn the secret to meeting the man of my dreams. Sadly, nothing I read, watched or listened to had the answers.

After doing everything I could think of I felt more despair than before I began my research. However, I knew I could not quit, because living without love for the rest of my life was not an option. So, I did the only thing I could think of; I dug *deeper.*

I thought back to one of my earliest childhood memories: After arriving home from church with the sister and my grandmother, I recalled twirling around in my "Sunday Best" – usually a lovely polyester pastel colored dress with a matching sash, black patent leather shoes and my har pressed and pulled up into a neat "Up-Do," – I used to pretend that *I was a princess.*

My childhood dream was that a strong handsome man (i.e., Prince Charming) would come along and sweep me off my feet. Fast Forward . . .

As I grew older my views about love and romance had not changed all that much as I still wished for a fairy tale ending. However, after becoming a mother, then married and divorced from first an abuser, then a cheater and lastly from an addict, my hopes of "happily ever after" vanished under harsh reality.

I did not get to have a fairy tale wedding and there were no dancing mice, flying teapots, or magic fairies to rejoice in my happiness. In fact, the only thing about any of my marriages that resembled a fairy tale wedding was the two words that appear on the screen after the credits rolled: "The End."

I contemplated a bit deeper about my previous marriages and I recognized there were some similarities between my ex-partners and my father. Similar to my ex-partners, my dad was abusive to my mother. He was unfaithful to women and he was an addict. Though I loved my father dearly, I found many of the negative qualities he possessed in my partners.

After reflecting on the past some more, I still was no closer to understanding why after countless years of trying to turn a "nothing boyfriend" into a "something husband," I was not saved from my circumstances, relinquished of my financial burdens, and living happily ever after with my children like a princess in some magnificent castle. That is when it hit me; the answer became clear.

Up to this point I had spent my life blaming other people; my ex's, my parents and even society for all my problems – including my relationship problems. *Especially* my relationship problems. I deluded myself into thinking that if I had a scapegoat to blame I would feel better about myself, but I only felt worse. I looked to other people to save me; I even found people that offered to "rescue me," but, in the end, there was only one message, one thing that became *crystal clear*:

No one was coming to save me.
I must save myself.

The one place I never thought to look for the answer to my relationship woes was within me. Now, I am not saying that every bad thing that happened in my past relationships was all me, or that I deliberately went out and asked to be hurt, cheated on or abused. However, what I came to appreciate was that my B.S. (Belief-Systems), played a role in my relationship decisions and choices.

After coming to some of these conclusions, I decided to explore some more possibilities that lead me down the relationship paths I had taken. Not because I was still in need of a scapegoat, but, because I wanted to be sure that the next time love came around, I would not need to be rescued, nor would I need to follow other people's rules or pretend to be someone I was not. I decided next time love came around, I would truly be ready. It was my responsibility to choose to "find my happily" without the ludicrous need for these cultural fairy tales that bore empty promises.

Could Disney Be to Blame?

Another thing I decided to explore in my quest to find the answers to my failed relationships was the role Disney's fairy tales played in my perspective. I began exploring movies and TV shows I watched. I wondered if Disney's, *Snow White* and *Sleeping Beauty* were to blame for my obsessive need to be rescued. After all, it was Disney who indoctrinated little girls like me into the rescue fantasy. Hell, they even assured parents that there were no reasons to be concerned with the stories being peddled to their daughters – all the while embedding messages that would later set most women up for "relationship suicide."

Disney's beloved princesses were certainly not the best relationship role models, particularly to young Black girls. Even the ever-present fairy godmother that showed up to prepare the princess to be rescued steered little girls in the wrong direction.

For the sake of not throwing Disney "under the bus" they have improved and adopted a modern-day message that empowers little girls. However, let's take a closer look at some of our all-time favorite princesses below so you can see some of the harmful traditional fairy tales pushed on women:

Beauty & The Beast's Belle: If at first you do not like him, spend more time with him until you do

While *Beauty & The Beast* is one of my all-time favorites it is also the one story that screams Domestic Violence! Despite the fact that Belle is beautiful, has a family that loves her and has a good head on her shoulders she winds up stuck in a castle with talking silverware and a ghastly beast that growls at her, throws temper tantrums, and, oh right, locks her in his massive castle. Definitely sounds like a classic case of D.V.

In the beginning, Belle stands up for herself demonstrating her wits and her independence. But, she eventually yields to the Beast's controlling ways. Hmm... I wonder, if it was this Disney story that led me into a violent relationship with man that not only stalked and abused me for years and separated me away from my family, friends and loved ones? Perhaps.

Cinderella: Wait to be rescued

This classic fairy tale of a young girl who was left to live with her jealous step-mother and step-sisters does everything from mopping the floors, cleaning the dishes and sweeping the chimney to mending her step-sisters dresses, fixing their hair and complimenting them in spite of how mean they were to her. She's practically a slave that does all she can to keep a roof over her head and avoid being thrown out onto the streets.

Finally, she hears about an opportunity that can rescue her from her circumstances, and in spite of all the things she knows how to do, she waits to be rescued first, by her fairy godmother – who by the way, gives her more restrictions and rules she must follow if she is to keep all the things she has given to her, and then by the Prince, who meets her and is head over heels in love with her, (and she in love with him). But, instead of breaking the rules her fairy godmother set for her, she takes heed to her warnings, and runs off into the night at the stroke of midnight.

Okay, I get it! No woman wants to be caught dead in their favorite comfy sweats, no makeup and their hair in a boring ponytail upon meeting a Prince. On the other hand, what are your chances of sitting around waiting for a man to show up with the perfect sized 8 Red Bottoms? I think you would be waiting a long time for that to happen.

The Little Mermaid's Ariel: The more you give up, the more he will like you

Ariel is a Disney character that came around when my daughters were little. While it was not a part of my generation the message was quite the same as all of Disney's other fairy tale stories.

Ariel, a beautiful mermaid that lives under the sea, falls in love with a handsome human prince named Eric. This story sort of reminds me of two people that come from different races or cultures and in spite of the distance or their differences, they fall in love and figure out how to make it work. Unfortunately, Ariel was neither patient or secure enough with herself to let the relationship unfold organically. Instead she finds herself in the clutches of an evil witch that casts a magic spell on her and she has to trade in her voice for a pair of legs.

She patiently waits for Eric to notice her, but not so patient as she only has a limited amount of time to win his love and affection before the spell runs out. She tried to "woo" him with her long gorgeous red hair, her bikini body and all of her physical attributes, because without a voice, that is all she believed she had to offer him. Eventually, (and just in the nick of time) Eric takes notice of Ariel and falls in love with her, but not before he winds up having to defeat the evil sea witch.

The message here ladies is to NEVER compromise your SELF for the sake of a relationship. Sure, there are healthy compromises one must make in a relationship. However, compromises should never be at the sake of giving up your values, talents or gifts for the sake of winning someone's affections. If you want a man to like you, let him see the real you.

Mulan: Be into everything he's into and eventually he will notice you

I think it is great to have things in common with your ideal mate, but then how far should women go to do that? According to Mulan she is willing to give up her female identity and take on the identity of a man to catch and keep a man.

I am all for being into sports or taking an interest in activities that men are into. However, one does not have to become one of "the bros" to hang with the bros. This is a very common thing that women do. They give up who they are and what they like and adopt all the things men likes in order to win their affection.

Even on dating sites, I've read some women's profiles claiming things like: "I'm into biking, mountain climbing, and I love sports!" And, while these things might be true, perhaps one should only include those things in their Bio if they intend on living up to those claims.

For men, not only is this type of behavior from women misleading, but if you do "hook a man," it will later create tensions in the relationship when you decide to show the real you.

Here's an idea! Be who you really are and spend time doing the things you truly love and he will either be into you or he won't. Self-respect is so much more attractive anyway.

Snow White: If you are trustworthy and pure, he will be too

Out of all of the fairy tale princesses, I am going to have to say that Snow White may be the fairest of them all, but she is also the naivest of them all. Not only does she get duped multiple times by the witch that happens to be her evil step-mother, but she also winds up living in a house in the forest with seven strange little men that fail to protect her. It is only when the Prince comes along that she is awakened from the witches evil spell.

The message here is that women are too dumb to take care of and protect themselves. Not the kind of message we want for our little girls, is it?

To summarize, here are a few examples of Disney's misleading lessons:

1. True love happens suddenly (*Little Mermaid*)

2. Prince Charming will be the best thing that will ever happen to you. You will not ever have to cook, clean or work for a living because Prince Charming will take care of all of your needs. (*Cinderella*)

3. A true princess does not have to learn effective communication because singing will solve all of her problems. Oh and yes, naivety goes a long way. (*Snow White*)

4. Once you are rescued you can ditch all of your family, friends and loved once (*Little Mermaid*)

5. It is okay to be locked away with a tyrant so long as he provides you with everything you need and want, and he takes care of your family (who by the way you will never see again) all for the sake of your company and your love. (*Beauty & The Beast*)

6. You can pretend to be somebody you are not and trade your beautiful voice in for a kiss. (*Little Mermaid/Mulan*)

The Truth Behind Fairy Tales

Would you be surprised if I told you that the real stories behind fairy tales that made our eyes sparkle and light up as children were filled with graphic violence, vengeance, jealousy greed, and incest? Where daddies preyed upon daughters, wicked step-sisters had their feet cut to pieces and naughty children slaughtered old people in their own homes? Sounds gruesome? Perhaps, but no more disturbing than the modern-day messages Disney spreads to little girls over the past decades.

I am not saying that all of Disney's messages were bad; some are good such as the old adage of good conquering evil. Nor, am I saying that finding viable answers to my relationship problems solves all my issues.

In my quest to discover the truth behind fairy tales I realize that real relationships do not involve knights in shining armor, "twin flames," a horse and carriage, castles and above all, living "happily ever after." However, the majority of Disney's "harmless tales" revealed underlying lessons that lead women to fantasize about being rescued, compromising first their values, then adopting unrealistic relationship expectations from other people and life in general.

You Are What You Attract

We live in a society that learns from and models one another's behaviors, good or bad, constructive or destructive. I know this because I and many of my friends were in exactly the same relationship boat. Sometimes better situations, sometimes worse. Let's take a closer look.

The Damsel In Distress

I began with one of my dearest friends, Lisa, who should be considered the poster child for Disney's damsel in distress – believing that one day a good-looking prince will rescue her, solve all her problems, and love her unconditionally (even though she falls short when it comes to truly loving herself).

Lisa hoped to meet a handsome prince someday. However, she also lived under the belief that if by some chance she was unable to meet and marry a prince, or if her prince was not charming, attractive or brave enough, that she would potentially be unhappy and have to struggle for the rest of her life.

As long as I have known Lisa, she was never in what I would call a committed relationship. Nor, had she ever had a "real boyfriend." At least, not one that ever stuck around long enough to be referred to in that way.

Lisa looked for love in all the common places that women search for love; in bars, night clubs and online dating sites. She even went to psychics who promised that "love would find her." Nonetheless, Lisa failed to meet a man that could fulfill her need to be rescued.

In the rare instances that Lisa would connect with a guy that stuck around, she managed to push him away by being too needy, clingy or by going way above and beyond the call of duty of girlfriend. It was as if she believed she needed to prove to men that she was worthy and deserving of their love and affection. Although in most instances it appeared as if her affection was more like smothering than cherishing.

Lisa seemed to live by Disney's altruistic adage that 'love conquers all.' She even went as far as imitating some of the characteristics of some of the Disney princesses such as: limiting her career goals, hiding her true feelings, growing her hair ridiculously long, wearing shoes that were two sizes too small, going on binge diets, and ditching all of her friends to sit around and wait patiently for Prince Charming to call.

Some of you reading my interpretation of Lisa might interpret her commitment and self-sacrifice as a noble gesture. Hell, for all I know, some men might find these qualities as worthy and deserving. All I know is that Lisa lived under the assumption that if she sacrificed her happiness, prayed hard enough, waited long patiently and suffered quietly her Prince Charming would see that she was "worthy" of being rescued. Far be it for me to argue. However, the fact is for as long as I have known Lisa, no matter how long she has suffered and waited and no matter how often she tolerated the intolerable, no one came. Her Prince Charming up to this point has been a no show.

When Harry Married Meghan

Most women over "Disney age" would argue that being a princess is really not all it is cracked up to be – thus denying their desire to become a princess that was rescued by a prince. However, I would have to disagree with all of you naysayers. Just look at all the Disney television and movie reboots and the world's fascination with the newly married Meghan Markle and Prince Harry. I read somewhere that *1.9 billion people* across the world tuned in to watch Prince Harry marry Meghan Markle. From what I read her wedding was a larger turnout than Princess Diana's and Kate Middleton's.

Women have been watching Disney's unrealistic princess with the tiny waist, pearly white teeth and her urgent need to be rescued for years. However, when Meghan Markle married Prince Harry she showed the world that a princess could also be an intelligent, independent, successful thirty-something divorcee, who is also a feminist from a broken home.

Women around the world *envy* Meghan Markle, wishing they could share her fate. Recently, many would say they even hate her because of her lack of gratitude for her status and position. However, what most women fail to see is that Meghan was not "rescued," nor did she win Harry's heart because she merely fantasized about being rescued then becoming a princess. Instead, Meghan was living her life fully and abundantly on her own terms.

I can already hear some of you screaming from the mountain tops, claiming how you read somewhere how desperately Meghan wanted to be a princess or how obsessed she was with Princess Diana, and so forth. *Whatever!* Trying to convince yourself that this was the reason, or that because she is famous, beautiful, and an overzealous overachiever she was lucky enough to wear the tiara will not make this belief true. For if your theories were true, all of us that wished to be a princess would be, and yet we are not – well some are, but not *all* of us. And, even if you are correct and your theories or beliefs about Meghan are true the bottom line is that she did not sit around hoping to get lucky. Nor, did she appear to have a need to be rescued when they met.

Meghan had her own life as an actress and an activist prior to meeting and marrying Harry. She continues to break barriers by demonstrating what life can be when an independent, happy, driven woman just so happens to marry a prince.

Mr. Stepford

Unlike my friend Lisa and some of the other women I know, I have never had a problem meeting men, nor finding a man to marry me. I dreamed of being rescued! But, I had no problem catching and keeping a man. I have been married a few times, proposed to a few times and in long-term relationships a few times. You do the math!

My friends would always tell me how lucky I was to have a boyfriend, or to be married to seemingly "perfect" guys. What they did not know (perhaps because I never shared) was how unhappy I was. Sure, I felt lucky enough to get married, have children and be fortunate to travel to exotic places, lavished with gifts and live in beautiful homes. But, because I was looking for true love, most of the relationships I was in felt more like I was settling until something, or someone better came along.

For instance, one of the loneliest relationships I had – and trust me there were others – was with a tall, handsome, educated successful man. Let's call him, "Mr. Stepford," as in *The Stepford Wives*, and here's why I referred to him as such:

Mr. Stepford is what most women would call "good on paper." He appeared to possess everything a woman would want in a man, (i.e., he ticked all the boxes on a check list). However, there was no true love between us. He said all the right things, looked the part and played the perfect partner, but inside he was empty, unemotional, and boring. He literally had less enthusiasm than my vibrator (yes, at the time I had a vibrator).

When I think back about Mr. Stepford I think I was attracted to him because I was trying to avoid some of the pitfalls and choices I had made in previous relationships. Prior to meeting Mr. Stepford my previous partners were poor, violent, unfaithful, or addicts. After dealing with these kinds of men, I figured I deserved someone that appeared to have all the qualities my previous partners had not. At the time,

I thought I had hit the jackpot. As though I had finally upgraded. Boy, was I wrong!

My relationship with Mr. Stepford was doomed from the start, only at the time I did not know it (perhaps deep down I did know it, and yet denied it).

Nonetheless, my nagging suspicions were confirmed after he and I went out to have drinks with his friend one night.

I must say, I was actually surprised when Mr. Stepford invited me to go out with him and his friends to this very sheik and trendy hot spot in Chicago. Everyone that was somebody was going to be there and I felt special that he had invited me to go, (as what I believed) was his date. Afterall, we were in a committed relationship, though you would never know we were looking from the outside in.

Once we arrived at the nightclub and everyone received the drink they ordered, Mr. Stepford and his friends began treating me as if I was some kind of groupie, basically just tagging along for the ride. I tried to act like I was not bothered by his behavior and instead set out to show him and his friends that I knew how to have fun. For some reason I got it in my head that I needed to prove that I could be sexy and desirable. It all went downhill from here.

I began doing what most women do when they go out of their way to "get a man's attention." I drank way too much liquid courage. *Bad idea!* I started with one drink, then two, then three, then perhaps four and before I knew it, I was boogying down on the dance floor with complete strangers, (most of them other single women). They seemed to all be vying for the same men's attention that I was.

I had not eaten anything all day and had a very low tolerance for alcohol. Eventually, after all the dancing and drinking and the drinking and dancing, I needed to make my way to the restroom. So, without checking in with Mr. Stepford and his stuck-up friends, I started off to the bathroom, but not before one of the women I was hanging out with grabbed my arm and decided she would join me. No problem, I thought. Women go to the bathroom together all the time. No big deal! It does not matter that she is not my Bestie or my sister, nor that I did not know her. I needed to pee, I was way past drunk and so off we went.

Once we were in the bathroom, which was one of those unisex hipster kind of bathrooms popping up all over the place, a stall opened. I began walking into the stall, seeing I was the next person in line, when all of a sudden Home-Girl from the dance floor barges into the bathroom with me. I'm like, WTF?

I was pretty annoyed with this Chick because like I said, she was NOT one of my Besties. However, my urge to pee was way more pressing at the time than my dire need for privacy. So, I lifted up my very, very short skirt and squatted over the toilet to do what I needed to do.

After I was done using the toilet, I got up and attempted to leave the stall so I could give her the courtesy of some privacy (which was more than she had given me up to this point) when out of nowhere she grabs me and pressed her body up against mine on the back of the bathroom door. At this point, I am really confused, but hold on ... It gets weirder.

While I am pinned up against the back of the bathroom door, she presses her lips against mine and then sticks her tongue into deep down into the back of my throat. Now, I have nothing against same sex love or women that are into that. I mean if that is your thing, do you. However, I was completely turned off. So much in fact, that my reaction (and all I could do at that moment) was to vomit!

Yep, I vomited. Not directly into her mouth, but all over her, the bathroom floor, the door and finally into the toilet. It was gross! And, can you believe that as I was puking my guts out, she started acting offended, saying, "That wasn't the reaction I expected! Was I that disgusting?" she asked. I stopped mid-puke, but still praying to the "porcelain god" to respond something like, "No, I'm sorry, I've never been kissed by a woman, it's not you, it's me. Really, I'm just sick, and I need to go."

Once I was back in the main room I scanned the room for Mr. Stepford and his friends. After spotting him, I walked straight over to him, explained the situation and told him that I needed him to take me home *right away*. Oddly, and without hesitation, he grabbed my hand, and we headed to the valet.

Mr. Stepford picked up his car from the valet and drove us home, stopping every so often for me to throw up on the side of the road. By the time we arrived at his house I think we stopped about ten times for me to puke. Keep in mind, he only lived about fifteen minutes away so that was quite a lot of puke!

When we arrived at his place I was doing my best not to throw up anywhere in the house. He had a very beautiful seven bedroom home located in one of the most prestigious suburbs in Chicago. High ceilings, Calcutta marble floors, a gourmet kitchen, and glass walls that framed the surrounding city.

To get to the master bedroom upstairs we had to take the elevator he recently had installed. Even though he seemed to appreciate that I was sick, I knew he would not be happy if I vomited anywhere except the toilet and even then, I was not sure he would be okay with that.

By the time we arrived at the master bedroom, to my surprise, Mr. Stepford was behaving much more nurturing and patient than I had expected. He walked me inside the bedroom, then to the bathroom where there he helped me take off my clothes. He then started the shower, placed me inside, then took his clothes off, got in and started bathing me. I thought the idea of him washing my hair and removing all the remnants of vomit would be weird, but somehow it was not.

After the shower he dried me off, walked me into the bedroom, and tucked me under the covers. I can earnestly say, (at least at that time) it was the first time that he made me feel loved and special, that is until he did what happened next.

As I lay in Mr. Stepford's bed I could hear him walking through the big house setting all the alarms, and lowering the blackout blinds. After he was done, he came back upstairs to the master suite and proceeded to lay down next to me, facing me and looking into my eyes.

I felt so ashamed and all I could do at that moment was apologize for ruining his night and getting so drunk. He did not respond and instead, as I turned to face my back toward him he began rubbing my back, then gently rubbing my head. It felt nice and I liked that he was being so kind and tender. But, no sooner had I had that thought when he slid up close behind me and thrust his penis into my vagina. Yep, just like that. No warning, no questions. He just started having sex with me, without my consent. And, what was worse, (if you can imagine it being worse) was that I was too weak and sick to say "no," or to stop him. So, I literally had to lay there, let him do what he wanted and when he was done, he rolled over and went to sleep.

I lay there for the rest of the night not saying a word, not even moving and after holding back the tears for what seemed like hours I softly cried myself to sleep. As I drifted off to sleep I wondered why this fairy tale romance and turned into nothing more an ill-fated tale or nightmare.

By morning I got up, dressed and made myself as presentable as I could, for all that it was worth. I guess he heard me moving about, because he awoke asking me if he could get me anything. "I'm good," I replied.

He talked to me about how "out of it" I was the night before and how he was really worried about me. Mr. Stepford said all the right things, and asked all the right questions. I brushed it all off, blaming the entire night "on the alcohol" and an empty stomach. "Yeah, that must be it," he said.

I am not sure who spoke next, but I found the courage to bring up the subject of him having sex with me after I was sick and throwing up. He seemed surprised by my questioning, but like a "proper gentleman," he proceeded to respond saying how he just felt so attracted to me, seeing me so helpless and vulnerable. His response almost made me want to throw up all over again. However, I kept my mouth shut and let him continue talking.

He went on to share how I was always so strong and how often he felt like he had to compete to "be the man" in our relationship. So, when he saw how vulnerable I was and how much I needed him, he felt a strong attraction to me.

After he spoke, I said nothing and felt as if I needed to pick my jaw up from the floor and remove the foot that had been shoved up my ass. *Why was I still sitting there?* I mean there was nothing more to say at this point and so I said the only thing I could say, and I thanked him. I thanked him for sharing and for taking care of me. However, the next day, after he left for a business trip, I moved all of my things out of his house, changed my number and cut all ties and communication, I have not seen Mr. Stepford since.

When I think back to that moment I realized that my desperate need to be rescued literally manifested a *rescue nightmare*. I still could not appreciate that after all the time Mr. Stepford and I had spent together that the only time he cared to show me an ounce of emotions was when I was at one of the weakest and lowest points of my life. This, of course, was a turning point for me, because I learned that no one was coming and I had to *save myself*.

I Tossed The Tiara

The day I decided to toss the tiara I became committed to loving myself wholly and completely. I began doing incredible things. Things that books like *The Rules*, and *Why Men Love Bitches*, do not recommend women do, such as: speaking to a guy first, expressing my thoughts, setting boundaries, not dimming my light for him to shine, and yes, calling him up and asking him out on a date if I wanted to do something.

I know that some of you may disapprove of my actions, particularly because it goes against everything that as women, we are taught to do, think and believe. However, the fact is the day I tossed the tiara out of the window — I gained the freedom to not only release and let go of my story, I learned to love myself and embrace my inner princess – no rules, no magic frogs and *no desire to be rescued.*

No One Is Coming; Save Yourself

From an early age, women are bombarded with images of a perfect romance with a fairy tale ending. Our heads become filled with the idea that our knight in shining armor will come galloping in on his horse to rescue us, but the truth is no one is coming, we must learn to save ourselves. That means not waiting for our perfect partner to come along to resolve our unpaid debts, emotional baggage, or any other area of our life where we are unfulfilled and unhappy.

Many women fantasize that someone will come along and rescue them from their problems and in some cases they even seek out someone to help them fulfill their fantasy, for example: behaving like the damsel in distress in the hopes that a knight in shining armor will swoop in, and seize the opportunity to rescue them, all before something bad happens.

However, unlike fairy tales I learned that real relationships take work, whereas meeting and marrying the man of your dreams is just the beginning. Learning how to love oneself, be open and communicate your wants, needs and requirements is the journey.

Having the occasional fantasy about being rescued is one thing; it's another thing to live with the proverbial premise that a "knight in shining armor" will come and sweep you off your feet. I'm not saying that we shouldn't strive for the love and relationship we truly desire or dream big. Just that, perhaps it's important to let go of the hope that one day we will be rescued and that if that happens, we can sit back, relax, and live "happily ever after."

CHAPTER THREE

The Beast

Prince Charming Is Not A Hero; He's a Myth

O nce upon a time, used to be my favorite fairy tale phrase. It filled me with lots of hope and anticipation that at any moment my Prince Charming would arrive. Nothing in my imagination could ever have prepared me for the truth; that Prince Charming was not a hero; he was a myth.

I expected Prince Charming to be picture-perfect, fearlessly conquering the world and slaying dragons with a badass sword for my honor. Inevitably, I ended up disappointed, believing that my Prince Charming was a "no show" because I was not pretty enough, or worthy enough for a man who was willing to risk his life for my honor.

The Beast

In the last chapter I mentioned how my favorite childhood Disney fairy tale was *Beauty & The Beast*. However, at the time I did not see Belle as a young woman that was sacrificing her freedom and self-respect, I saw her doing what she needed to do for her family and for love. Perhaps it was this fairy tale story that led me to enter into a relationship with an angry beast that never became a Prince.

I was only sixteen years old when I married a man no older than myself. I was already a young single mother to a little girl and I yearned to provide her with a loving nuclear family. In the beginning, The Beast I married was charming, particularly to my daughter. However, similar to the character traits of Disney's Beast, he began to throw temper tantrums, became very controlling and made every attempt to lock me up in our home away from my family and friends.

Our first home was a small apartment in the Bronx in a very poor neighborhood. Far from the magnificent castle that Disney's Belle was trapped in. Nonetheless, I made every attempt to make the best out of my humble circumstances and to be a be kind, loyal, and loving wife and mother. My hope was that if I possessed the qualities and traits of a princess one day my beast would turn into a Prince who would love me and my daughter. Sadly, *that never happened.*

Instead, over the years the beast I married became even more controlling and physically abusive. He controlled where I went, what I wore and who I spent my time with. He beat me daily, forced me to have sex with him, spit on me, and shamed me. Eventually, the violence would escalate to a point that forced me to flee and never look back.

Nearly two years into my marriage to The Beast I became the mother of another little girl and at that point, the abuse was so bad I had to flee and run to stay in a shelter. However, one day I needed to run errands in the city so I took my daughters to stay with one of my aunts (who for some reason told the Beast where I was and that she had my daughters who I left in her care for the day.)

Just as I was wrapping things up and headed back to my aunt's house, I received a call on my mobile from a number I did not know. Since my aunt did not have a phone, I answered it because I thought it might be her calling me from a payphone. To my surprise on the other end of the line was The Beast, to which I was surprised because I had not given him my new number. According to him, he picked up my daughters from my aunt's house and told me I had to come to where he was if I wanted them back. Although I was frightened to meet him, I was more afraid of what he might do to my little girls if I did not.

I agreed to meet him at our old apartment in The Bronx, which was directly across the street from where my aunt lived. Although I did not feel safe meeting him there, I figured it was close enough for me to run to my aunts for shelter if anything went wrong. When I arrived, he was standing on the street in front of the building with my sister-in-law's husband, which was very surprising considering the two of them never hung out nor were friends.

A part of me was happy there was someone else there, sort of like a witness (though having a witness never stopped him from abusing me).

I walked up to The Beast and immediately asked for my children (who were not standing with him). He then ushered me into the building and told me they were in the apartment. I asked why he would leave them alone in the apartment and he told me that they were asleep and he did not want to wake them.

The apartment I used to live in was a refurbished old tenement apartment with large rooms and wooden floors. There was lots of light that poured in from all the windows facing the street, however it did not have a warm cheery feeling like sunlight often brings into a home.

Once inside of the apartment my sister-in-law's husband walked into the greater living area, leaving me and The Beast standing face-to-face in the foyer near the front door. I figured it was best to stand closest to the door in case I needed to run out of the apartment. I told him that I would wait by the door while he went to wake the children and bring them to me. That is when he told me that he had killed the children and that he was going to kill me and then kill himself.

My heart sank at what he was saying and I did not want to believe him, yet I did not want to challenge what he was saying. Instead, I stood saying nothing, tears strolling down my cheeks. That is when he reached into his pocket and drew out what looked like a carton of Newport Cigarettes. "So, now you are going to have a smoke? Since when did you take up smoking?" I said. "I don't smoke," he responded, reaching into his other pocket and pulling out a small caliber gun.

I watched as he opened the cigarette carton and pulled out two bullets, loaded the weapon and pointed it at my head. "Look," I said, "I realize that you are not happy and that you hate your life, but I don't want to die."

"Well, that's too bad," he replied. "Because you're going to die and then I am going to kill myself."
Believing that my children were dead and seeing no one was coming to save me, not even my sister-in-law's husband who stood staring out of the living room window, while he smoked his cigarette. So, I got down on my knees and began to pray. That's when the gun went off and things went completely black.

I cannot say how long I lay there on the hard wood floor, but it must have been a long time, because when I awoke it was nighttime outside and the room was dark. I tried to be quiet because I was not certain I was alone. I then crawled to the front door and let myself out and ran. Never looking back.

I ran to my aunt's house to tell her what happened and when I arrived my daughters were there. I hugged them tightly, then I ran to a nearby payphone to call the police to tell them what happened. Of course, by the time they arrived, searched my place and determined the threat was gone, they did nothing.

I told them I wanted to file charges. I was quite surprised when they responded with the same things they always told me, "Mam, we have no evidence to support a crime was committed here. No one has seen or heard anything accept you. We can go arrest him if we find him, but we cannot hold him."

"There's a bullet hole in my apartment and you still cannot do anything?!" I asked. "Perhaps, something would have been done if the bullet was lodged into my head, when he aimed the gun and shot?"

"Well, that would be unfortunate, but yes, if he commits a crime then we can arrest him."

I wish I could say that was the last I saw of The Beast, but it was not. I had nowhere to go and no one could save me, not even my family, or the police. I felt trapped, because no matter what I did and in spite of how much love I showed him, my love did not transform this cruel beast into a loving Prince.

When I think back to the very first moment the Beast hit me, I think how I "should have" run and never looked back. But, I was young and confused as to what was actually happening. It did not make sense to me that a sweet and kind man could suddenly turn into a cruel monster.

So, I brushed off the first time he hit me, then the next, and I allowed myself to believe him when he said the reason he hit me was because he loved me so much, and that he was afraid of losing me. I also believed him when he told me that if I left him he would find me and he would kill me. He proved the latter by his actions.

This story might seem romantic to some women, having a man so smitten with you that he would rather lock you up in his home to have you all to himself. However, the moment your freedom is threatened or you become isolated from the people that not only love you, but that might influence your decision making, is the moment you are a victim of abuse. Sure, people can change and do change and yes, there are instances whereas bad people become good people. However, I learned first-hand not to wait for the abuse to stop, nor accept relationship abuse in any form.

In the end, I escaped and got away from The Beast I married, though it nearly costs me and my children their lives. Escaping was not without consequences nor regrets. In the end I had no love for him and I recognized the monster he is. My hope in sharing this short story, my story, is that it can help you choose a different path and avoid this fate.

The Dancing Beauty

I had a friend named Diane that was also in and out of abusive relationships. However, looking at her no one would ever believe that a woman as beautiful and intelligent as she is would ever end up with men that would cheat on her, or verbally and physically abuse her. Then again, abuse has very little to do with the victims looks or intelligence.

It all began many years ago, when Diane started dating a guy named Doug. From the outside looking in Doug seemed perfect for Diane. Not only did everyone think he was "good on paper," but we genuinely believed that Doug was Diane's Prince Charming. He was kind, smart, attentive and funny. Everyone loved him! And, most of all, Doug seemed to really love Diane.

After Diane and Doug had been dating for a year or so he asked Diane to marry him. A group of friends had all gotten together for dinner one night at Doug's request, so he could propose in front of all of Diane's friends and family. We were all so excited for Diane! I thought to myself, finally she was getting the man she really deserved.

I remember at one point turning to look at Diane, as Doug proposed, and recalled how unhappy she looked. At the time I chose not to say anything and brushed it off as nothing more than shock or surprise. But, as the weeks passed I would soon learn that there was much more to Diane and Doug's sordid story.

Not long after Doug proposed, Diane called to tell me that she had called her engagement off. I pretended that I was surprised, though I was not. Because there was something about the night Doug proposed that did not quite settle right. Still, I was not quite sure why Diane was not happy the night Doug proposed, so I asked her to tell me what lead to the break up.

As Diane began to share what happened, she started by telling me about her past and the hard life she had lived. She talked about some of her past relationships and how often she had been lied to, cheated on and or abused by men. Yet, in spite of all that she went through it all and she remained optimistic about love. She did her best to never blame anyone new in her life for the pain that past lovers had caused. So, when Doug proposed, she said it was the "happiest day of her life."

Diane wanted to be sure that she and Doug had a good marriage. She explained how she knew so many friends, some of them her family, that had bad marriages, that she did not want to be one of those persons. She told me that the things she believed ruined most marriages was *secrets*. And, so that she and Doug had no secrets between them or anything to hide (not even from the past) she decided to open up and be more transparent about her past life. Diane had already shared most of the things from her past. But, just so no secrets from the past could affect her future, Diane wanted to be sure that Doug was sure about who she was before they married.

According to Diane, Doug did not like talking about the past and lived by the credo that, "the past is the past," which made it difficult for her whenever she tried to share some of the intimate details about her past. However, now that she and Doug were going to be married, Diane told me how she insisted that Doug listen. This time, she said, he finally did.

Diane began telling Doug about *everything* in her past. She told him about being molested when she was a kid and why the thought of having children made her feel afraid. She told him how when she was fourteen, she ran away from home and worked as an exotic dancer to make ends meet. She told me how she and Doug talked for hours, with him mostly listening and by the end, he thanked her for sharing and told her how much he loved her. He also asked her to give him some time to digest everything she shared. Diane agreed, and was actually happy that he had listened and that he was actually going to think about all that she had shared. She was scared to lose him, she said. But, she was more afraid to go through a marriage filled with secrets.

A few days had past when Doug finally called Diane to thank her again for sharing and he told her that he still wanted to marry her in spite of everything. Diane expressed how overjoyed she was to hear this --- that was until the next day when she and Doug had what she described their last meal together.

Doug invited Diane out to eat dinner at a very romantic restaurant to celebrate their engagement. He said that he wanted it to be just the two of them. Everything was going well, except for the fact that Doug kept flirting with the waitress. Something Diane said he had never done before. The first couple of times, she said that she played it cool as if it did not bother her. But, after the third, or maybe the fourth time, she decided to quietly confront him and let him know how uncomfortable his flirting was making her.

According to Diane, she asked him if he would stop. Doug laughed it off saying how Diane was making a big deal out of nothing. However, after he could see how serious Diane was as she was not laughing with him he looked at her with this cold, blank-look and said, "Look, if I can get over all the shit you shared with me, and ignore the fact that you were a stripper and a fucking whore, then you can deal with a little harmless flirting."

Diane said that she was in shock. Not necessarily by what Doug said, though she shared what he said hurt, but, it was more so the *tone of which he said it*. All Diane said she could do at that moment, was take off her engagement ring, slide it across the table and quietly walk out of the restaurant. Not once, she said, did she look back.

After Diane shared her story, I wondered if she could ever live down her past and not just in Doug's eyes, but in the eyes of any man. However, Diane did not feel as if she had to be ashamed of her past. She said she could live with society judging her for the stepping stones she took to make it through the world. What she would not accept was a man that claimed to love and care about her and judging her for the rest of her life.

While a part of me felt devastated about Doug and Diane's breakup, the other part of me felt very proud of her for standing up for herself. Yes, I wondered if she and Doug could have talked it over or tried to work it out. Perhaps, she wonders the same thing. But, at the end of the day I think she did what was best for her at the time.

All too often, I see so many women spend their entire lives looking for their knight in shining armor only to find that Prince Charming is not a hero, but a myth. No woman ever thinks about what happens after Prince Charming and the Princess go home to live happily ever after. Nor, do we think that the Prince that shows up at our door might not be as charming as he leads us to believe. Perhaps, all we can really hope for is a man with faults and imperfections like our own.

Shining Armor

Sandy and I met while we were working at the same little dive bar on the island. We were both finishing up our last semester of Nursing School. It was not the most ideal working situation, but it paid the bills, the tuition and provided a flexible work schedule.

Like most of the women that worked at these kinds of establishments, Sandy yearned for a better life. I know this because every night at the beginning of our shift she would say how tonight would be the night her Prince Charming was going to walk in the door and save her from the "shithole" we worked in. I always thought there were better ways and certainly better places to meet a man. Until, one night while Sandy and I were at work her knight in shining armor walked in.

In walks Steven. A young, not so hot looking guy who had lots of money. He looked more like a Napoleon than a tall handsome Prince, because he was very short, loud and arrogant, and far from tall, dark and charming. Nonetheless, Steven seemed smitten with Sandy following her all around the bar, and showing up for every shift she worked.

One day Steven finally got up the nerve to ask Sandy for her number. Well, that is not exactly true. He actually had his weird looking friend with the missing front tooth ask Sandy for her number because he thought it would look uncool if he asked. Nevertheless, Sandy reluctantly gave up her digits, Steven called her, and her life changed.

Sandy and Steven became the couple everyone envied. In fact looking from the outside in no one could quite understand what Sandy saw in Steven. He had crooked teeth, was loud and unattractive. Nonetheless, Sandy became very fond of Steven, and for several years they seem to live "happily ever after."

After a couple of years of dating Steven invited Sandy to move into his beachfront home. It was a far stretch from the small studio Sandy lived in so she happily accepted. Eventually they would move in two small dogs, followed by two cats. Life for the two of them seemed good.

During Sandy's final semester of nursing school she started telling all of her friends about some major changes she noticed in Steven. She talked about how late he stayed out and how he started drinking more than usual. She shared how she tried to talk to him about her concerns. However, he ignored her concerns and insisted she focus her time on her studies rather than what he was doing with his free time.

Sandy, decided not to push because she did not want to rock the boat, or like they say in Hawaii, she did not want to "make waves." However, she could not shake the feeling that her now perfect life was going to come crashing in.

Over the next couple of months Sandy became more convinced that Steven was cheating. She talked about how disconnected and secretive he was behaving. But, the worst part was that every time Sandy would confront him he would threaten to put her out on the streets. She did not know what to do.

On the one hand, she did not want to lose Steven. On the other hand, she did not want to be put out on the streets, especially while she was so close to earning nursing degree. Sandy said that she refused to live with a man who chose to keep secrets or threaten her security and safety. Therefore, if she had to end the relationship or leave Steven she would do that.

Sandy did not have any evidence to prove that Steven was cheating so she decided to do what most women might do in her situation and began looking for evidence to support or contradict her speculations. She hoped that she was wrong, and that she was simply overreacting or being insecure.

She loved Steven, and for the most part she was happy. She just could not shake the feeling that something was not right. So, she prepared herself to deal with whatever she found out. "Time would tell," she said one day. However, the time would come sooner than she thought. But, time did not reveal what Sandy thought it would.

Sandy began investigating Steven quietly, trying not to "rock the boat". Since she was sure if Steven was cheating she started her search by going to all of Steven's known hangout spots. Then she visited his favorite surf spots and the local bars he liked to go. Lastly, she would arrive home earlier or later to see if she might catch him at home with another woman.

After all of Sandy's snooping she came up empty. So, she decided to give up her cause and to leave well enough alone. However, just when she had convinced herself that she was the problem Steven's behavior got worse.

Steven started staying out all night and inviting some shifty people over to their home. She knew nothing she said was going to change his behavior. Confronting him would only make things worse. So, she waited for him to slip up, or come clean.

After a night of drinking Steven arrived at their home behaving more belligerent than the previous nights. However, just as Sandy was going to confront him, he dropped something on the floor that looked like a mobile phone, but not the mobile phone Steven usually carried. He scrambled to pick the phone up from off the floor. But, before he could do so, Sandy grabbed it and picked it up.

At first Sandy assumed Steven lost or broke his other phone. But, when the phone rang the look on Steven's face told her otherwise. Sandy answered the phone and on the other end of the call was a woman's voice. Sandy asked who the woman was and the woman replied that she was Steven's girlfriend. She then asked the woman how long they had been together and the woman stated that they had been dating for a few months and that in fact, she was pregnant. The woman on the phone then proceeded to ask Sandy who she was and she wanted to know where Steven was. Sandy was stunned, but not surprised, did not say a word and simply passed the phone to Steven.

Steven took the phone from Sandy and in a low voice began speaking to the woman on the other end of the phone, telling her that now was not a good time, and that he needed to call her back. Sandy, said she did not say a word to Steven and simply walked slowly to their bedroom, grabbed her backpack and books, walked out the front door and drove off in the car Steven bought her. Steven ran after the car as Sandy pulled off, calling for her to stop and come back. She did not stop. Nor, did she ever look back.

Later, Sandy shared how angry and afraid she felt, mostly because she was penniless and had nowhere to go. The good thing was that she had graduated from nursing school and that meant she would not have to go back to work at the dive bar, or be out on the streets for too long. Most people would say that Sandy's current circumstances looked grim. However, Sandy said deep down she knew that eventually she would be just fine.

Prince Charming Is Not A Hero

There are hundreds of amazing women all across the world, some of them we know and many of them we can agree are exceptional. They are witty. They are beautiful, and they even partake in social causes to help make the world a better place. Yet, sadly many of them end up with guys that do not value the love they have to offer.

Sometimes we see the red flags and ignore them. Other times we compromise our joy and our happiness in hopes of living happily ever after with a Prince that rescues us from all the bad things that can happen.

However, there comes a point when our own personal happiness has to mean more to us than the "happily ever after" facade and when a new guy enters our lives and seemingly with all the answers to our prayers, we must be prepared to ask ourselves the right questions, such as:

Is this guy looking to take care of me, and buy me gifts other than getting to know me and spend time with me?

Or, does he insist on using money and gifts to rescue me from my circumstances whilst not actually putting any personal value into the relationship?

If so, we might be dealing with a guy who wears the shining armor, but by no means is he willing or capable of stepping up to be a true Prince.

The Carriage Ride Home

There was once a wealthy guy named Leonardo and while no one knew how he acquired his wealth everyone knew that he owned some of the most beautiful properties in the world.

Leonardo was also the only person any of us knew that had his own personal cook, butler and a chauffeur that would take him about town. He was also known as a bit of a playboy or a "Ladies man" as my grandmother would call him, because he was always seen about town with a different woman every night of the week. He could be seen at any of the swanky restaurants wining and dining some of the most exotic women and at the mall or boutique stores taking them shopping.

One night I had the chance to meet Leonardo, on a night when my Bestie and I decided to stop for a drink at a downtown bar before going to see the Motley Crew in concert. Definitely not my first pick, but hey that's what best friends do, right? Anyway, we stopped to have a drink because we thought it would be cheaper to have a couple of drinks before the show, rather than purchasing drinks at the stadium. No sooner had we sat down to have our drinks when Leonardo, who was sitting alone at the bar, walks over to me and my friend and introduced himself.

"I'm Leo," he said. Of course we already knew who he was though neither of us said so.

"Are you going to the concert?" He asked. "If so, I have a couple of extra stage passes if the two of you are interested in joining me." How presumptuous, I thought. But, before I could respond, my friend blurted out, "Sure! We'd love to join you."

I tried to shoot her the side eye as I felt like we at least needed to know what his offer involved. But, my friend who was gleaming kept on yapping and replying on "our" behalf.
"Did you two drive?" He asked.

"No!" She exclaimed. "We took a taxi, just in case we wanted to drink." Good lord, I thought. Will she ever shut up?! Why not tell him everything and all our plans for the week while you're at it?

"No problem,' he replied. "We can walk over to the arena together. Then my driver can drop the two of you home after the concert if you'd like." Yippee! I thought condescendingly.

"Wow! That sounds awesome," my friend said gleefully smiling.

Since there was no time for my friend and I to discuss our plans for after the concert and since I did not want to ruin what was seemingly turning into a good night, at least for her I thought, I went along with the plan.

However, I could tell this was going to be an interesting night, but I was not prepared for the journey the long carriage ride home would bring.

There was something about Leo that told me not to trust this guy. It was not anything he said or did, because up to this point he had been pretty nice and generous. I guess you can call it a women's intuition (wink).

By the time we arrived at the concert, Vince Neil was already performing and falling out drunk across the stage. Still, it was a great show. I suppose you can say it was extra special because we also got to meet Tommy Lee and Nikki Sixx, after the show. I guess having backstage passes had its perks.

After the concert, we thanked Leo with a big cheerful hug and headed toward the arena exit. By the time we arrived in the parking structure his driver was already waiting for us. From the outside it looked like a long black 10-seater Lincoln Navigator. Only once you got inside, the back seats were completely removed and reconstructed to look more like Austin Powers "Shag Pad" than a mode of transportation. There were cool pink lights around the roof and floor and a full-sized bed with fluffy pillows and surrounded by a bar. My instincts told me not to get in, to run for my life! Instead, I did the same thing I do when my Uber driver shows up and looks like a serial killer and got in anyway.

Leo asked each of us for our home addresses so he could text it to his driver whose name was Tony. In hindsight, I wish I would have planned to get out of the vehicle at my friend's destination, or had her get out at mine. But, for some reason I said nothing and simply gave up my home address.

Thinking back, I thought Leo was interested in my friend, who was a beautiful brown skinned Thai Woman, with long hair down to her butt. I also did not want to appear rude or insulting, after he so generously gave us VIP backstage passes to the concert and offered us a ride home. I tried to sit rather lay back and enjoy the ride, but the long carriage ride home would not be the cozy coach made for a Princess.

By the time we arrived at my friend's place, she climbed out of the car, thanked Leo again for being so generous, and she kissed me goodnight. We were not down the road two minutes before Leo, who was suddenly pressed on top of me, started kissing me all over my face and neck, telling me how hard he prayed to have a Black girlfriend one day, as if I was a collector's item Barbie you cannot find on a shelf.

While I was disgusted and surprised, I was more pissed at myself for not getting out of the vehicle with my friend. I now found myself in a car alone with two men I did not know. *Stupid!* I thought. I knew I had to think quick so I said the one thing I could think of to get him off of me.

"Wow," I said. "Thank you for telling me how you feel. I'm flattered. Unfortunately, I have my period and I'm a pretty heavy bleeder."

He suddenly stopped doing what he was doing, moved far enough away from me to see if I was lying and stated how disappointing that was. As if he really thought I was going to fuck him in the back seat of his mobile "Shag Pad." The nerve!

Since I didn't want to make things even more awkward than they already were I tried to be nice and offered to go out with him another time, when I was not on my period. I told him that I also found him very attractive and said that if I did not have my period I would have given in right on the spot. I thought that by mentioning my period over and over again he would get turned off, but to my surprise he asked me for my cell phone, typed in his number and called his phone with it to make sure he had my number.

"There! Now I have your number. I'll be traveling to Tahiti for about a month, but when I get back I will take you up on that offer," he said.

Gawd, I wanted to puke! But, instead I agreed and thanked him for his "kind" offer.

As the carriage pulls up to my house I thought that would be the end of it, but instead of him letting me out and saying goodnight, he got out of the vehicle with me. He said he wanted to walk me to my door so he would know where I lived and use the bathroom if that was okay. "Sure," I said, "but just so you know I didn't have time to clean the bathroom," which was totally a lie and it didn't work because he insisted that he did not care.

I slowly opened the door and as I let him in, I made sure not to close the door behind me just in case I needed to run out. He looked around my place, which was pretty small compared to the homes he lived in and he complimented me on my decoration skills. I quickly pointed him in the direction to the bathroom. When he came out he smiled, thanked me and then kissed me on the cheek. I walked him to the door, let him out, locked the door behind him, and then watched from the window as he and his driver rode off. I did not really sleep that night for fear he would show back up at my door.

The next morning I called the friend from the concert up to tell her what had happened and she was yelling excitedly into the phone about how lucky I was that Leo had taken an interest in me. Most women, she said, would be "so lucky" to have a rich guy be so into them. I didn't agree with her and told her how much of a creep I though he was. All she could say was how she wished it was me that got dropped off first so that she could have a chance with him. I do not think he would have wanted you I told her, because according to him, he has been searching for a Black girlfriend. Which would exclude her since she is Asian.

A few months had passed since the Leo incident, when out of nowhere he called my phone. Since I had never bothered to store his number in my phone, or for that matter change my phone number, I had no idea who was calling when I answered.

"Hey! It's Leo. How are you?" He asked. "I'm doing well," I said. "But, I'm actually in the middle of something. Can I call you back?"

"No need. I'm actually calling to apologize. I've been back for a few months and I didn't reach out sooner because I was so ashamed of my behavior that night after the concert. I'm not sure what came over me, but all I do know is that my behavior was completely inappropriate and I wanted to call to apologize. I'm also hoping that if you accept my apology you might also accept a dinner invitation, on me of course, and you can drive yourself to be sure nothing happens. I'd like to officially apologize in person."

"Well, that's very kind of you Leo," I said. "And, I appreciate your apology, however I've already put the whole thing behind me so please do not feel as if you need to do anything else. Your apology is enough."

"Does that mean you won't take me up on my dinner invitation? If you say no, I will forever have to walk around town feeling ashamed and believing that this was the last impression I left on you."

"Well, I'm not turning you down because I am harping on things, I'm really just super busy," I said.

"Please, let me take you someplace to have a nice meal and then make an official in-person apology. I won't take no for an answer!"

And, it was that last statement that I was afraid of, that he would not take "no" for an answer. He knew where I lived and he was still harping on the issue. Whereas, at this point, I was simply trying to move on with my life.

Since I wanted him to go away and leave me alone I reluctantly agreed to his dinner invitation. *I know, I know, stupid, right?* But, at the time I figured if I met with him in a public place and I let him make amends I could avoid him showing up at my front door with flowers. So, we decided to meet during the middle of the week at one of the only French restaurants in town. Of course, I drove myself.

At dinner he ordered a bottle of red wine, which he mainly drank, and we ate a five course French meal. During dinner, neither of us brought up the incident. I realized that at this point I found myself *wanting* to believe that his behavior really was out of character that night, thus making it easier for me to forgive him and move on. I did not feel so comfortable with him that I would want him to drive me home. However, I was willing to give him the benefit of the doubt, that was until he showed me all the reasons why I should not.

After dinner, he paid the bill and I thanked him for a lovely evening. He walked with me to the parking garage, then he offered to walk me to my car, which happened to be parked on the second floor of the parking structure. He insisted that since it was late, he'd walk me to make sure I got into my care safely. He didn't want any "creeps" to jump out and get me – *go figure*. I agreed to let him walk me because I felt certain he wouldn't try anything stupid in a public place. Unfortunately, I was wrong!

As soon as I put the key into my car door he pressed himself up against me from behind running his hands up and down my skirt and over my breast. I tried to turn around, but I could not because he literally had me pinned against my car door. But, when he finally released me and gave me enough space to move from under his clutches I pushed him off of me.

"What's wrong," he exclaimed. "I thought you liked me? You said the next time we saw each other we'd be together and that the only reason you didn't fuck me that night was because you were on your period."

"Are you serious?!" I yelled. "I only said that so you would get off of me and wouldn't rape me!"

"Rape you? Are you serious? Why would I need to rape you, or anyone for that matter? Do you know how many women I can be with right now and yet I'm here giving you the time of day? You should be so lucky that I am willing to call you one of my girls. Your stocks just went up honey. I guess you're one of those ungrateful stuck up Black bitches I've heard about, that doesn't know a good thing when she sees it. That's why you Blacks do so poorly in life because you do not know how to be grateful for anything. Well, all I can say is that after hanging out with you, I see no need to pursue having a Black girlfriend. If Black women are anything like you I can do without."

"Well," I said, "I thank you for your honesty and thank you for not being interested in me or other Black women. I'm sure we will do well without you. At this point, I am going to get into my car and drive home. But, if you make any attempt to touch me, call me or come by my house I am going to show you just how much you will regret fucking with 'Black bitches' like me. Now, excuse me so I can leave."

He stepped aside, sort of in shock by the nerve of me and I got into my car and drove off. I was shaking and it was not because I was afraid, but angry. Angry for not listening to my inner voice, following my instincts and for letting my guard down around someone who I knew was not someone to be trusted.

When I think back to this moment I realize that perhaps somewhere deep inside I wanted to believe that I was worthy of being courted around in a coach by a Prince. However, the lesson I learned is that while it might look like a fairy tale carriage from the outside, it still might just be a pumpkin being pulled around by some filthy rats.

Prince Charming Is A Myth

Meet Prince Charming! The one that we have all been waiting for. He's tall, handsome, not to mention, rich, and he has the solution to all of our problems. He is here to save us, tackle all of the challenges we face. But, wait... There's more! He is willing to give up his entire kingdom and make all our dreams come true. Destination - *Happily Ever After!*

CHAPTER FOUR

The Glass Slippers

If the Shoe Doesn't Fit, Do not Force It

In the fairy tale about Cinderella, her fairy godmother used her magic wand to turn Cinderella's rags into a beautiful gown and gave her a pair of glass slippers to wear to the ball. Tis one of the glass slippers the Prince later found (after Cinderella fled the ball at midnight so not to be found in rags).

The next day the Prince announced a wide search throughout the kingdom to find the girl who won his heart, using the single glass slipper throughout the village to see who the shoe belonged to. Finally, coming upon Cinderella's home he was able to match the shoe to its proper owner. It was not long after that the two of them had a splendid wedding and went on to live happily ever after.

But, how many feet had been offered up before its rightful owner had been found?

According to the story, we know that prior to Cinderella trying the shoe on that her two step-sisters tried on the glass slipper, (and according to the version you read) as did her evil step-mother. But, the shoe did not fit. What we do not know is how many days it took for the Prince to find the maiden whose foot would fit the tiny glass slipper? Nor, how is it that no other maiden in the entire kingdom fit the same size shoe as Cinderella? Did Cinderella have special sized feet? Was her foot bound and stuffed into the shoe? Or, could it be that the Fairy Godmother simply made the shoe a custom fit?

The story about Cinderella demonstrates the cultural impact found across some African, European and Asian countries for women to have tiny feet. In some cultures, big feet equates to ugly, clumsy and unattractive (similar to Cinderella's mean stepsisters). Whereas women with small feel (like that of Cinderella) are considered more beautiful and well-bred. This is also the case in China where foot binding is still practiced and it is becoming more common in America where women are choosing to undergo selective "Cinderella Foot Surgery" to "make their shoe dreams come true."

The Shoe Fairy

When I was a little girl the last thing I wanted was to have big feet. My sister (who is now five feet tall tops, compared to my five feet and five inches) always had what my aunts would describe as small, cute little feet. I was not wearing the same size seven and a half I wear today. Still, I felt as though my big feet were larger than my sisters and for that matter, larger than the average little girls' feet my age.

Once a year my grandmother would take me and my sister shopping for a new pair of shoes and every year I would argue the reasons why I did not need a new pair of shoes. I was determined to convince my grandmother that my feet had not grown and to prove I was mistaken my grandmother would always call over the shoe salesman, a.k.a. the "shoe fairy," to measure my feet with that metal foot measuring tool, called the

Brannock Device. FYI, I did not learn the name of that tool until I began writing this book. Better late than never for useless information.

Anyway, I was determined to do everything not to go up a shoe size. Even if that meant I had to forgo a new pair of shoes that year, which I was willing to do if I had to (FYI I would not forgo a new pair of shoes today).

The moment the shoe fairy put that measuring device under my foot, I would curl my toes under and press down hard onto the balls of my feet so that my foot would appear smaller than it actually was. Imagine a ballerina's foot for a minute and that's pretty much what I was doing – squeezing the toes together, and standing on my tip toe. Ouch!

Every year I tried this trick and every year the shoe fairy would bring out a half size up. However, one year my trick must have worked because my shoe size stayed the same! At that moment I felt like a princess whose Fairy Godmother had granted her wish. Or, perhaps my feet did get bigger, but without knowing I was practicing some form of foot binding. If you were to look at my feet today you would notice that my toes are much smaller compared to the rest of my foot!

Nevertheless, at that time I did not care if my foot looked deformed. So long as I did not have big feet. Which also meant, that I might still have a chance at someday snagging a Prince.

As I grew older I realized the size of a woman's feet had nothing to do with the kind of man she attracted into her life. There is no shoe fairy and no one is coming to wave a magic wand to turn you into someone you are not. Women with smaller feet have just as many challenges as women with larger feet, and vice versa.

The takeaway therefore is for us to learn to love ourselves for *who we are*. However, if we decide to subject ourselves to pain in order to change our perceived flaws, let us do it under the name of self-improvement, instead of the guise of misplaced vanity. After all, the very thing we do not like about ourselves may be the one quality that places us "a foot" ahead of the rest.

If The Shoe Doesn't Fit, Don't Force It

Every woman envisions that moment a man places a glass slipper upon her feet, thus solidifying their love. However, if the shoe doesn't fit, don't force it. If you have to walk down the aisle to live happily ever after in ill-fitted shoes and blisters on your feet is it really worth it? Maybe, it is best to find the shoe that fit's just fine and have the courage to walk away. Otherwise, you will wind up stumbling around, trying to play the part in a role that just does not work, which, is exactly what happened to a dear friend of mine named Nancy.

Nancy was not the kind of woman that men fawned over. In fact, most people did not even know Nancy existed until she decided to be seen. Like most women, Nancy hoped that one day she would meet her Prince Charming. However, her belief was that in order to get the prince she needed to "act as if," i.e., compete against other women and then look, act and dress the part in order to win the guy over by any means necessary.

Nancy started meeting and dating rich guys after she was invited to hang out in a new social circle. Previous to hanging out with the "upper class" group of friends she began spending time with, Nancy wore her hair in a high ponytail, wore flip flops and surfed on her days off. Because Nancy was serious about living a more luxurious lifestyle, she decided to trade her flip flops in for a pair of stilettos.

You might be wondering why Nancy had this sudden change of heart or rather lifestyle. Was it that she was getting older and wanted to settle down? Or could it have been a broken heart that sent her on this trajectory? The answer is the latter.

After Nancy got dumped by this guy she really liked named Lindon, she decided it was time to step up her game. Lindon was a school professor from a pretty well to do family. Every summer Lindon would travel from Hawaii to the Hamptons to teach tennis and spend time with his family and Nancy's hope was that one summer Lindon might invite her. Sadly, Lindon had other plans and they did not include Nancy.

One day after Nancy got off of work she went over to Lindon's place for a visit. He had just gotten home from surfing and so after letting Nancy in he went to hop in the shower. Nancy spent a lot of time at Lindon's place and decided to make each of them a drink while he showered. That is when she noticed the long blond hair.

Nancy, who was a pretty slender brunette, knew the hair did not belong to her. Lindon wore locks and was only blonde because of the sun. Nancy's heart was racing and while she did not want to ruin the good thing she and Lindon had going she decided she was going to confront him and confront him she did.

As Lindon came out of the shower and into the living room where Nancy sat waiting she decided to address the long blond hair before she lost her nerve.

"Who's the blonde?" Nancy asked Lindon who was standing in front of her toweling off.

"How'd you know about that?" He responded, not denying there was a blonde.

At that point, Nancy decided to go along with Lindon's presumption that she knew more than she did.

"Are things serious between the two of you, or what?" She asked.

"Well, they cannot be that serious," he replied. "Otherwise you wouldn't be here now would you. Why are you asking all of these questions about Karen? What are you stalking me or something?"

"Stalking you!" Nancy exclaimed. "I do not need to stalk you or anyone else. I thought we were seeing each other. I had no idea you were into seeing anyone else. So, where did you and Karen meet?"

"I know her from New York. She flew into see me."

"Oh, so I guess you two are going to be hanging out when you go to the Hamptons this summer?"

"Probably. Why are you asking me all of these questions all of a sudden? You never took an interest in my private life before. Why now?"

"Wow!" Nancy said. "I guess I thought I was a part of your private life. I had no idea I was ... Well, what am I to you anyway since now you are letting me know that I am not a part of your private life?"

"Look Nancy, do not ruin a good thing. We are having fun. Why complicate things with titles and labels?"

As Nancy listened to Lindon babble on about *how not serious they were*, it was at that moment, Nancy decided to stop being the girl that everyone had fun with and become the woman every man cannot live without.

I could totally relate to Nancy's pain and frustration, even her need to change things up in her life. What I did not agree with was the path she had chosen to find her happily. Nonetheless, the journey she decided to take was hers alone so I said nothing and simply wished her the best.

Since Lindon chose a Hampton's girl over Nancy, at least that is what she believed, she was now hell bent on proving to Lindon that she was just as good as a girl from the Hamptons. Her belief was that rich people lived for the finer things in life -- the finest wines, designer clothes, the best cars, and the biggest houses. And, while Nancy did not have any of those things, she was determined to do what she could to look the part.

Nancy started her journey at the largest shopping mall she could find. She then applied for credit cards at Neiman Marcus and Bloomingdales, and purchased a couple of dresses, shoes and accessories. Next, it was onto the hair salon, where she had extensions put in. And, lastly, she went to MAC Cosmetics to purchase some makeup.

By the time Nancy did her hair and makeup and put her clothes and her red bottom stiletto on, which she complained made her feet hurt, none of us recognized her. She was already a beautiful woman, but now she looked the part for the role she was about to play. The only thing she needed to do was find a place to find her Prince.

Since most of us lived on the country side of the island, none of us knew where the "Townies" (people that live in Waikiki or Honolulu) actually hung out, let alone rich Townie's like the ones Nancy was looking for. Nevertheless, Nancy did not concern herself with minor concerns like this and instead, she hopped in her SUV and drove to town to meet her Prince Charming.

After Nancy drove around town for hours, she finally valeted her car at this very upscale restaurant in the heart of Waikiki. Although she could not afford to valet and buy herself a drink, she decided to pay for the valet because the idea of walking through the parking structure in her stilettos was unthinkable. Also, her hope was that someone would offer her a seat and perhaps buy her drink once she was inside and that is exactly what happened.

Five minutes after Nancy walked into the restaurant a hot guy named Ken walked up to her and offered her a seat and a drink. Nancy wound up at Nobu, a hot new swanky sushi restaurant that had a DJ and cocktail lounge on Saturday nights.

Ken spotted Nancy the moment she walked in the door. According to her, all the eyes were on her as she walked in. But, only Ken got up from his table and invited her to join him and a group of friends that were enjoying cocktails at one of the tables in the room. Nancy took Ken's arm, which he placed out for her to grab hold of and he escorted her to his table. She was grateful for his arm because her feet hurt so badly and she was not sure she would be able to take another step.

According to Nancy, all of the men and women at Ken's table were well dressed, good looking and seemingly well to do. After Ken introduced himself and everyone at the table (though Nancy could not remember any of the names) everyone said their hello's and continued on with their conversations. No one treated her as if she did not belong and she had a good time.

Nancy learned that Ken lived part-time in Hawaii and part-time in Los Angeles, where he claimed to have worked as Mel Gibson's stunt double. After Googling Mel Gibson's stunt double, we later found that to be a lie, but that's another story.

Ken seemed like a nice guy and seemed rather eager to invite Nancy into his world. He seemed to have friends in high places. He knew all the politicians on the island, all the club promotors and the nightclub and restaurant owners.

After spending time getting to know Nancy, Ken invited her into his inner circle, which included mansion parties with indoor waterfalls and heated swimming pools and house parties filled with party favors not meant for children. For Nancy it all seemed very exciting and surreal. That was until Nancy's magic spell began to wear off.

After Nancy and Ken were seeing one another for nearly a few weeks he invited her to a party at his Hollywood Hills home in Los Angeles. She was very excited about going, particularly because she thought the invitation made things "somewhat official" between her and Ken. Unlike Lindon, who never introduced her to any of his friends, nor invited her off the island to the Hamptons. Ken seemed pretty open about who he was and welcomed Nancy into his world. Or, so she thought.

Nancy flew to Los Angeles on a Saturday afternoon. The party was scheduled for Saturday night. She took it upon herself to arrive early so she could acclimate herself and spend some quality time with Ken before the party. She figured he would be busy preparing for the party and she wanted to be available to help him with any last minute details he might need help with. Ken was all too happy to take Nancy up on her offer to help, which only lead Nancy deeper into believing there was something more between the two of them than there was.

When Nancy initially arrived at Ken's place he asked Nancy to run errands: pick up his dry cleaners, his Lethal Weapon Jacket and several other errands he said his housekeeper did not have time to run. Since Nancy flew into LA, she did not have a car. So, Ken gave her the keys to his brand new Jag to get around the city.

This led Nancy to further convince herself that Ken would only do something like this if he was A) into her, and B) believed she came from the upper class. Sadly, Nancy would learn that neither of these assumptions were true.

By the time Nancy arrived back at Ken's place with his jacket, flowers and other slew of items Ken sent her to pick up Nancy had less than a couple of hours to get dressed. There were caterers and staff all over the place. However, Ken was nowhere to be found. So, Nancy decided to make herself at home by carrying her things into one of Ken's spare bedrooms to get ready.

Nancy was so excited about the party, particularly the outfit she brought to wear. She wanted to make a great first impression for Ken's friends and prove to them that Ken made the right decision in "choosing her."

From what the invitation read, the attire was "California Casual," which Nancy had no idea what that meant. I know this because while she was shopping she called me to ask me what California Casual was. I told her that she should ask the sales associate because I did not know. However, she was too embarrassed to ask, believing that they would judge her for not knowing.

After a couple of hours Nancy was dressed and ready for the party! Her outfit included a pair of jeans, a silk blouse, some accessories and her red bottoms that hurt her feet.

Her hair was styled in some big barrel beach wave curls and her makeup was light, stating that she was not trying but just naturally beautiful.

As Nancy stepped out of the bedroom the house was filling up with women dressed in knits, flowing silks, and cocktail dresses. The men were dressed in nice jeans or silk slacks and a sport coat. It was at this point that Nancy realized she was very underdressed and there was nothing she could do about it, because it was all she had to wear.

Nancy made her way around each of the rooms searching for Ken, but she could not find him. She texted him a cool, "Hello," to which she received no response. She rang his mobile. Still no answer. Finally, she asked one of the staff where he was and was directed out towards the pool.

Ken's three-story home featured four bedrooms with balconies overlooking an outdoor pool and surrounded by beautiful landscaping that included succulents and exotic plants. Most of the guests were socializing outside near the fire pits, while other's picked food from the exquisitely catered spread. By this point, Nancy was tired of looking for Ken, so she decided to make her way to the food. However, just as she was making her way through the sliding glass door, she bumped heads with Ken, who was holding hands with some buxom blonde.

"Hey! You enjoying the party?" He asked Nancy who stood stunned and flabbergasted.

"Yes! Great party." She said trying to hold back the cracks in her voice. "I um, left all of the things you asked me to pick up in one of your bedrooms, and I set the keys back in the desk drawer you told me to grab them from."

"Awesome! Thanks a lot, Love." He replied.

"Are you Ken's new PA?" Asked the buxom blonde.

"His PA?" I asked confused.

"Personal Assistant," she blurted out laughing.

"Oh!" I replied holding back the tears and pretending to laugh along.

"No Gina!, she's a dear sweet friend of mine from Hawaii. I invited her to see how we party in The Hills."

"Oh! How sweet! Well, I hope you're having fun. Hope we get to catch up with you later." She said tugging on Ken's arm. "Come on Honey, we gotta go do that thing."

"Right!" He says to her. "Have fun, Hon. Let's catch up when I'm back in Hawaii," he said kissing Nancy on the cheek.

Nancy, stood stunned and frozen in one spot for what seemed like hours. She wanted to run back to the bedroom, grab her things and leave. However, her feet hurt so badly that she was barely able to walk. Also, she felt like if she went up to the room too soon, she might run into Ken and Gina and the thought of that made her pain feel worse.

Nevertheless, after some time, Nancy made her way back to the bedroom, packed her things, called an Uber and left outside the front gate to wait. As her Uber rolled up she got in tears spilling down her cheeks. However, she would not allow herself to cry, not at least until she arrived back at her hotel room, which she luckily booked just in case.

She stepped softly into her hotel room trying not to add too much pressure to her sore aching feet. She then sat on the edge of the bed to pry off her ill-fitting red bottom shoes from her aching feet. Her feet were swollen with red blisters forming across the tops and bottom of her feet. Even as she sat with her shoes off, the pain was still too unbearable for her to even walk.

After Nancy sat for some time waiting to ease the pain in her feet, she made her way over to the vanity, and began wiping away the makeup from her face. After she was done, she made her way to the bathroom, showered and then made her way to the bed, all the while thinking about the night, particularly Gina's question, until suddenly something on the floor grabbed her attention.

"Ouch!" Nancy cried out after stubbing her foot as she reached across to pick up one of her red bottom shoes. She then noticed something about her shoes that she had not noticed before. Her regular shoe size was a comfortable size eight, or an eight and a half if she required more space for her wide foot. However, the shoe she held in her hand was a size thirty-seven (which converted to an American size six and a half or seven).

She sat bewildered for several minutes feeling foolish for spending over a thousand dollars on a pair of shoes that did not fit. She realized that like her shoes, her new friends were simply not a good fit. And, that forcing herself to be someone she was not in order to "fit in" was as unpleasant as walking a mile in a pair of shoes two sizes too small.

Walking A Mile In Glass Shoes

Would you cut off your toes in exchange for marrying a Prince?

Or, would you choose the perfect fit for you?

Society convinces women that they have to scheme, compete and change who they are in order for the perfect man to ask for their hand in marriage. And, if by some chance they are not lucky enough to walk down the aisle in a pair of glass shoes by the age of thirty, they would somehow be deemed unlovable.

Cinderella met the qualification, became the princess and went on to live happily ever after because...the shoe fit. However, most women are stumbling around trying to play the part, never realizing that the role *just does not fit.*

"Finding your happily" is not going to happen with blisters on your heels or your toes scrunched up tight – or worse, your feet cut off! And, by chance if you happen to nab the Prince and walk a mile or so in glass shoes, you will only end up miserable with broken glass piercing into your feet.

The Perfect Match

I used to be the kind of woman that men called pretty, but never "hot" and that men would marry, but then cheated on. I felt undesirable and found myself praying to GOD for a man that would choose to love me over all others.

Anyway, as I mentioned in Chapter Three, I was "lucky" enough to marry a man that loved me, so much in fact, he would knock me upside the head, drag me across the floor and isolate me from everyone I knew just to prove how much he loved me.

Of course, this was not the kind of love I had in mind for myself. So, instead I began to imagine a love that would be much kinder. So, I sought to meet a kinder gentler man. Someone polar opposite to **The Beast** I had previously married. However, he too would take his love away and while he was kind to me, he was also kind to all the other women he was sleeping with. Come to think of it, he was having sex with everyone but me. I guess he thought he was doing me a favor.

Years later, after earning my Bachelors of Science in Nursing and after spending many years single and alone I decided to try online dating. However, I must admit the idea of looking for love over the Internet was quite daunting. Nonetheless, I gave it a try, thinking it might be easier to find love online than in a bar. Boy was I wrong!

I tried three different dating sites: **Plenty of Fish**, because it was free, **Match**, because it was not free, and **eHarmony**, because I thought it was the only site for serious people looking to meet and marry their match.

If you have tried online dating then my experiences will resonate with you. However, if you have never tried online dating or dating apps, then my experiences might frighten you, but do not let it. I'll talk more about how I can help you with online dating in the coming chapters.

Let me begin with **Plenty of Fish**. Well, the name speaks for itself and I should have taken the name as a red flag. Also the fact that it was free to use the platform was a bad sign. But, I did not get too wrapped up in these minor, but very telling details. I told myself I was giving online dating a try and therefore was going to try the site for free to see how I liked it.

Setting up an online dating profile on **Plenty of Fish** was rather easy. In fact, too easy if you compare it to **eHarmony** or **Match**, which I will get to later. You answer some short and easy questions about who you are and what you want, load a pic and voila – "You've Got Mail."

The day after I created my **Plenty of Fish** account I opened it up to find nearly a hundred responses. I was certain it was mistake, or some sort of error until I began reading the messages:

"Hey sweet thing, great pic. Is that really you?"

"Wow! I cannot get over how hot you are, are your pictures real?"

After reading about twenty, or more messages that had the same theme I got the idea that the photos I uploaded must have looked fake. I will admit the pics I shared were professional shots. However, I was trying to enhance my chances by putting my best face forward. According to Google it is best to include a desirable headshot for your profile pic. So, that is what I did. Unfortunately, every guy seemed to believe my profile pic was a fake.

The next day I decided to change my profile pic to something more natural. I also included the professional pic as an alternative pic so guys would see my different looks. Later that day when I looked at my messages, there were even more responses than the first day. I did not really want to read all the messages I had incurred, but since I was serious about meeting someone I decided to start reading.

However, the next batch of messages was worse than the first:

"Wow! You are F***ing Hot! Why do not you me a call so we can hang out. (555) 555-5555 Jeff"

"Hello, my name is Mark. I hope I do not offend you by asking, but are you really a girl?"

"Dude, you are hot! Are those pics real or are you a man?"

After reading half of the messages from men asking me whether I wanted to have sex with them, or whether I was a man, I decided to close my account with **Plenty of Fish**. I began to wonder when people mentioned how much I looked like my father, if what they were really saying is that I looked like a man. Needless to say, my self-esteem was shot! But, since I was determined to meet someone I tried again, this time with **Match.com**.

Match.com seemed a bit more serious than **Plenty of Fish.** They offered two options, free profile, or a subscription. I decided to go with the paid options since I had such a horrible experience with **Plenty of Fish's** free service.

I filled out my profile information and answered a general questionnaire. I felt a bit more optimistic since the questionnaire on **Match** appeared more detailed than it was on **Plenty of Fish.** After I was done filling everything out I logged out and waited for my account to be approved.

The next day I received an email from **Match** saying that I could begin searching for matches. I was super excited, particularly since I heard so many people talk about their great experiences. Upon logging in I noticed less messages than I had received on **Plenty of Fish.** I think about five to be exact. I began reading the messages hoping to be pleasantly surprised, but was sadly disappointed:

"Hi, my name is John. I read your profile and you are beautiful. Would you be interested in meeting for a cup of coffee or something?"

Since John's message did not come off as vulgar or anything I decided to read his profile before responding. His subject heading read:

"Love to travel. Successful MD. Avid hiker. Who are you?"

Not bad, I thought, although sparse. I decided to read his responses to the questionnaire to see if we had anything in common.

"Never married, not interested in marriage or children. Looking for flings or casual relationships. Interested in women who are White, Latin, or Asian. Smoker. Drink five times per week. Not into books prefer movies."

After reading his entire profile I realized we had absolutely nothing in common, as I was previously married, had children, not looking for a hookup and I am Black. According to his interest I am not even on his list of options! I decided to not respond to John, and instead moved onto the next message:

"Hi, Jason here. I'm not usually into Black chicks, but you're really beautiful."

Next!

"What are your plans this weekend?"

Chuck!

"Hi, I came across your profile and we seem to have a lot in common. I love to read, love to travel, am a father to a young son

and am on here for serious dating. I'd love to learn more about you." Robert

Finally, something that sounded a bit more promising! Perhaps things were looking up. I decided to read his full profile. It read: *Recent widow, father to a young son and looking to meet my soulmate.*

A widow! My initial thought was that he killed his wife, which is why he was now a widow looking for a new mom for his son (I used to watch a lot of Lifetime Network shows). However, after reading his summary and his questionnaire responses, I decided to reply.

"Hi, Robert,
Thank you for your interest. If you read my profile summary and questionnaire then you know that I was previously married, a mom and a nurse. I like traveling, swimming and hiking. I am also passionate about social causes and believe in volunteering to help make the world a better place."

The next day I logged onto **Match** excited to see if Robert messaged me back, and he did.

"Hello Collette. Nice to meet you. Yes, I read your profile and you seem like a lovely woman. We seem to have a few things in common, which is great. How long have you been on Match?"

I have to say that I was unimpressed by his response. Although, I am not quite sure what I expected. I think at the time I was hoping he asked for my phone number, or was willing to share his so we could talk and get to know one another. But, that is not what happened.

Instead, over the next few weeks, all Robert did was send me messages through **Match.com**. He never asked for my number, or asked me to meet him for a cup of tea, coffee or anything. He simply sent me messages everyday asking me how my day was and shared how his day was. Eventually, I got the feeling I was writing a "Pen-Pal," only we would not send one another stickers, or write letters to each other with scented pencils.

After four weeks of sending message back and forth over **Match.com** with Robert, I decided to pursue other prospects on the site. The problem was, while I was receiving messages from time to time, Robert was actually the most promising.

Nevertheless, instead of giving up or throwing in the towel, I decided to be proactive and start searching through the profiles. After all, I was an able-bodied woman that was capable of initiating contact or asking a guy out, regardless what "The Rules" say. However, just as I was prepared to begin my search, I got a chat message from Robert that read:

"Hi, are you up for a chat?"

I was quite surprised to receive a chat message from him so it took me a moment to respond. It was as if we had gone from first base to second and I was not sure I was ready seeing all we ever did was send email correspondences through the site. I decided to respond:

"Hey Robert," I said. *"This is quite a surprise. Sure, I'm open for a chat."*

"Sorry I've been a bit distance or preoccupied. I would have loved to already met you in person, but I am out of the country with my son."

"Really!" I replied. *"I had no idea you were out of the country. What country are you traveling?*

"I am currently in the Middle East. I came here for my son to see my deceased wife's family. Only a couple of days ago my son had an accident and is now in the hospital and in need of an emergency operation. Unfortunately they will not accept my insurance here and I do not have access to the kind of cash they need to save his life. I need your help. Can you wire ten thousand

U.S. dollars. I will pay you back as soon as I get back to The States."

I sat staring at the cursor on my computer for what felt like an eternity. For one thing, I could not believe that Robert thought I was foolish enough to wire money to a complete stranger and secondly, I could not believe I was that foolish to waste my time messaging some guy over the Internet for a month!

I did not bother to reply to Robert. Instead, I closed my account and took a yearlong break from online dating. I decided to try meeting men in person. I thought at least it would be easier to gage whether someone was serious about dating, married, or a liar. Then again, I realized I was wrong about that assumption, as I met my previous partners in person and one was dating other women and the other was a liar.

It would be nearly a year before I ventured back to online dating. And, in all honesty I only gave it another try because a good friend of mine, a doctor I met at working at a Miami hospital, said that I should give online dating another try.

According to my friend, the only site he felt was worth trying was **eHarmony**. He said that he received quality matches daily and although he had not met anyone he would walk down the aisle with he was pleased with the experience thus far.

That night when I got home from work I signed up on **eHarmony**. Well, it was not actually that easy to sign up. The entire process takes about an hour or so, at least it did back when I signed up. I am not sure what the experience is like now.

Apparently, **eHarmony** developed an online application for people looking for marriage or serious long-term relationships. All I needed to do was create a profile with all my details and answer a lot of questions to create a personality profile. Evidently, the information I shared with them would help them to screen my profile and provide eligible and compatible matches. They claimed to be able to remove ninety nine percent of the non-compatible users to make the online dating experience more enjoyable, save time and more successful.

I had nearly completed answering all of the questions and was just wrapping up the final question, which asked something like: "Where would you prefer to meet your match?" And, since I wanted to keep an open mind and enhance my chances at meeting my perfect partner, I chose the option that read, "Anywhere in the world." I figured it was best not to be too picky, as well as maintain balance when answering the questions.

I cannot say for sure how long it took **eHarmony** to tally up my responses, but however long it took, the reply I received was not what I expected.

After giving up nearly two hours of my life to create a personality profile on **eHarmony**, the response they gave me stated that they did not have any eligible matches in their database for me. In other words, they were not able to match me with *anyone in the entire world.* **The entire planet? Seriously?... Give me a break!!!!** That was the final straw for me. I was convinced that online dating was simply not for me.

The next day I went to work and told my doctor friend of my experience. He told me to wait a few weeks and try again. Apparently the same thing happened to him the first time he signed up. Evidently, I needed to be more precise with my responses and less in the middle. And, so six weeks later I tried again and gained access.

The way **eHarmony** works is they send you a number of matches each day. And, if one of your matches selects you and you select them you will be able to answer more questions that eventually open the communication between the two of you. I imagine meeting a match on **eHarmony** is more challenging than trying to gain access into Fort Knox.

In the beginning most of the matches I received were pretty good. However, none of the matches were interested in communicating with me, so the communication was closed. However, after a month or so later I went out on my first date with one of my matches and here's how that played out:

Stephan seemed like the perfect match. He was successful, funny, kind and had a good sense of humor. We spoke briefly on the phone once, but then he recommended we meet somewhere in person to really get a sense of one another's personality. I chose to meet somewhere close to where I lived, but nowhere I frequented. I figured if he was a weirdo I would never have to see him again, purposefully, or by accident.

I arrived about a half hour ahead of schedule to meet him at this hotel bar nearby where I lived. It was public enough, yet quiet enough to have a first date conversation without it being awkward. Stephan arrived on time and looked just like his picture, tall, dark and handsome. Unfortunately, he was not impressed with the way I looked as the first comment he gave me was about how much shorter my hair was than my picture, and how much taller I appeared in person. Mind you he was over six feet tall and bald (and not on purpose). I explained how I had just got a new haircut from my best friend who was a stylist and that I chose to wear heels, since he said he was six feet two inches tall.

We decided to order a drink and sit near the bar to get to learn more about one another. The conversation really flowed and things seemed to be going well, until he got on a hot topic surrounding politics and religion. I rolled with it since everything was going well, at least in my mind it was. But, apparently Stephan disagreed, because the next thing I knew he was referring to me as a conservative Christian. I was shocked, since I was not a conservative, or even anything close.

After about an hour or so we wrapped our date up and said goodnight with polite pleasantries. I went my way, and he went his. I had no intension of reaching out to him again, nor of going back onto **eHarmony** for that matter.

Online dating reminded me a lot of fishing which I enjoy. However, judging my lack of success I realized at the time I was not good at either – fishing or dating. Even in the rare instances I had the right bait, i.e., I looked the part, and had the right equipment to "catch and keep a man," it would be years before I would catch what I was fishing for. Instead, I learned that while there are **Plenty of Fish** in the sea, in order to find the perfect "**Match**," you have to first be "**inHarmony**" and balance with yourself.

CHAPTER FIVE

The Mirror Never Lies

STOP BLAMING OTHERS; PICK UP A MIRROR

In the fairy tale about Snow White the Magic Mirror reveals the qualities the Queen needed to possess in order to be the "fairest in all the land." Unfortunately, the Queen was either unwilling, or unable of developing the qualities she needed. So, instead she sought to destroy Snow White because of the qualities she possessed.

In modern times many view Disney's *Snow White* as a form of typecasting older women as evil, jealous "old hags." Whereas, their much younger counterparts are seen as innocent, perfect and pure. While we are taught that beauty is in the eye of the beholder, or that true beauty begins and ends within, the media puts out a lot of propaganda on what the standard of beauty should be (particularly in America).

However, not every person and/or culture accepts, or identifies with these standards. Let me share with you a personal story to show you what I mean about looking in the mirror:

"Mirror, mirror on the wall, will he choose me after all?"

The Skinny Mirror

As a young girl I could relate to the story of Snow White, as I too was naïve, trusting and hung around a bunch of trolls. Unfortunately, the trolls in my life were not always there to help or guide me in the right direction. In fact, many of them teased me for being skinny, which in my mind equated to ugly and undesirable.

By the time I grew into a young woman I had heard every skinny joke you can think of:

"You're so skinny you can dodge raindrops."

"You're so skinny you can be a poster child for 1-800-HUNGRY."

I had very little confidence, particularly in the way I looked. While all of the girls I grew up with had blossomed into women with thick round hips, I still resembled a skinny young girl, only by the time I matured my breast were much larger. I looked nothing like the young women in my community. There was no one I could look up to, or that reflected the image I would see when I looked into the mirror.

By the time I got married to my first husband I somehow believed that he married me because he loved me, or at the very least thought I was pretty.

However, after he began beating me day and night and referring to me as a "Black ugly crackhead" that should be so lucky to have a man (as if beating my ass was doing me a favor), I realized even that was not so. I was ugly even to my own husband.

I would spend the majority of my young adulthood doing everything I could to gain a pound or two. I ate constantly and stuffed my face with fast foods, desserts, or anything fried. I even ate bags of flour, drank **Ensure Nutritional Drinks** and sought help from my doctor to help me gain weight. People treated me as if I was some kind of freak or a monster just for being thin.

Having children did not make it better and in fact, things only got worse. Prior to the man I am married with today, my previous husbands treated me as if I was a charity case, whereas I should *be so lucky* to have a man, even if that meant they would physically beat me, steal my money, neglect me and my children or sleep with other women. All of this to say, I had very little confidence in myself. All I saw when I looked into the mirrors on my wall was a weak skinny woman that was not pretty enough to receive love or respect.

My lack of confidence in myself led me to believe that if I gained weight I would be construed as beautiful. At the time I believed this I was eating a lot of crappy food and taking medication from my doctor that was allegedly supposed to help me gain weight. However, one day all of these drastic measures I was taking to gain weight would catch up to me.

I have two younger sisters. One day my sister closest to me in age and I were on the subway to go shopping in the city for new shoes for my daughters. A few weeks prior to this trip my stomach had been upset. However, I attributed the pain to all the stress I had been under due to my abusive marriage and having to relocate into a shelter for battered women.

Since I had not been experiencing too much discomfort a couple days before I felt like it would be safe to travel. However, all of a sudden I had the urge to go to the bathroom and I am not talking "number one," I am talking "number two."

The urge became so unbearable that I suggested we exit the train several stations prior to our destination. I remembered leaning in to whisper in my sister's ear, "When this train stops I am going to bolt off of this train and head to the nearest toilet I can find." My sister, who was looking at me bewildered by what I just shared and shook her head to acknowledge what I told her.

If you have ever had an upset stomach that gave you the runs then you will probably relate when I said it took everything in me to not crap all over my pants on that train. So, by the time the train pulled into the station, I took off like lightening, running off the train, up the stairs to the street level and desperately searching for the nearest place I could take a shit!

Sadly, New York City is not the easiest place to find a public bathroom, given most of the business do not offer their customers the use of their toilets. So, I did the next thing I can think of and took my chances.

I ran into a record shop that sold vinyl records, CD's and tapes. I scanned the place for someone to help me until I spotted a young Latin guy come up from behind the counter.

"Can I help you," he asked. "Yes," I said frantic. "I *really* need to use your bathroom."

"Sorry, we don't have a public bathroom."

"Listen, I really have to go and not number one, but number two and if you do not let me use your bathroom RIGHT NOW, I am going to take a crap right here on your floor."

"Okay, lemme see what I can do. It's not very clean though," he said.

"Sir, I really do not care. I feel really sick and I *really* have to go!" He led me down a short hallway, down some steps and into a dark dingy little bathroom. "Thank you!" I said, pushing the door shut behind me and barely getting my pants down before relieving myself while I squatted over the open toilet.

Once I was done using the toilet, I washed my hand and made my way back into the main room to thank the guy that let me use the bathroom. When I made it out I saw my sister standing in the shop with tears streaming down her face. She was worried about me, but not more worried than I was for myself.

My sister and I decided not to shop for shoes after the ordeal and instead of taking the subway home we took a taxi back to the Domestic Violence shelter where my kids and I were staying.

The next day I made an appointment to see my doctor about my condition, which only worsened over the next several days. I had diarrhea for a week straight and was unable to eat anything without having to go to the bathroom.

The doctor could not explain my condition and attributed my symptoms to stress and the ordeal I was going through. However, he explained that severe digestive disorders like I was experiencing can result from Domestic Violence and trauma. So many abused women endure dreadful health consequences that are connected to the stress from the emotional and physical violence.

He recommended I "change my circumstances," which was easier said than done. However, just in case, I discontinued the weight gain medication, stopped eating crappy food and decided to give up my weight gain journey. At the time, this was the only thing I felt like I had any control over.

Not being able to eat, or digest food properly made me quite aware of a few things: The first thing I learned was that in order for me to fix what I did not like on the outside, I needed to work on what was happening on the inside. The second revelation was how much my childhood traumas and the domestic abuse played a role in my low self-worth and even my health being endangered.

I cannot say that these revelations I had cured me of my insecurities, as I carried this story about myself for a long time. Even today, I can become triggered about my weight, particularly when someone references my how "thin looking" I am.

However, I know that in these instances, I need to do some inner work and some deep introspection. I have learned that what I see is merely a reflection of my own thoughts and beliefs.

Everyone will see something different when they look into the mirror. However, we think very little about how what we see is not always what is actually there, or is it?

Some of you reading this might not understand why anyone would get teased for being construed as too thin or skinny, particularly if you are not a part of the Black or Brown community. However, beauty standards are based off of community, family and societal programing.

Similar to Snow White's evil Queen, I was projecting an image that was not reflecting back what I wanted others to see. My belief was that I was ugly, undesirable, and therefore unworthy of love. Therefore, the image I projected out to the world reflected back who people on the outside would see.

The Mirror Does Not Lie

When you look into the mirror do you believe the mirror reflects back the truth, or a lie?

Many years ago when I was on my quest to find love the one place I had not thought to look was within me. That was until I was challenged to do the Mirror Exercise for ten days. During the Mirror Exercise you stand in front of a mirror, look deep into your own eyes and repeat positive affirmations to yourself.

I had never done anything like this before, however the church that I was attending offered a self-esteem class and challenged everyone to try it. Here's how the experience played out:

Day 1: On the first day I wrote down a list of positive affirmations. Some I took from the list I was given and some I created for myself. My affirmations I came up with were:

"I am beautiful"
"I love myself"
"I am worthy of love"
"I accept myself"

After I wrote down my affirmations I stood in front of my vanity and began to say my affirmations out loud, all the while looking deep into my own eyes.

"I am beautiful, I love myself, I am worthy of love and I accept myself."

The goal was for me to repeat the affirmations to myself five times in the morning and five times in the evening. However, I was not able to make it past saying it to myself three times in the morning before I burst into tears.

Day 2: I woke up in the morning, brushed my teeth, washed my face and began my morning affirmations:

"I am beautiful, I love myself, I am worthy of love and I accept myself."

Again, the same thing happened on the second day that happened on the first. I burst into tears before I could finish saying the affirmations five times.

Day 3 and **Day 4** were the same as the previous days.

However, by Day 5 something changed;

Day 5: By day five I did the same thing I did every morning, however this time I hopped up on top of the vanity counter and while looking deep into my own eyes. I placed my arms around my chest and holding myself tightly, I said the affirmations to myself as if I was speaking to someone else.

Here's what I said: *"Collette, you are beautiful and you are worthy of love. I love you and accept you wholly and completely."* I repeated this to myself five times and although I cried worse than I did the previous few times, I felt better than I had the days before.

The next week when I returned back to the class I was taking at my church we were asked to share our experience. And, while I was not really prepared to share all that I had experienced, I wanted to ask a question so I raised my hand.

The pastor responded to my raised hand and asked me to stand. I stood, but quickly acknowledged that I had more of a question than a share, and he permitted me to do so.

"I did the Mirror Exercise every day for a week and every day I cried because I felt like everything I was saying to myself was a lie."

The Pastor thanked me for sharing my question and then replied:

"The reason you believe that the affirmations you are saying to yourself are lies is because you have been living under the story of other lies that were not true. You will have to convince yourself of the truth, which is that you are a child of GOD and that you are loving and worthy of love. Believe this and repeat it until this becomes your truth."

The whole room was silent, as was I. However, I completely accepted and resonated with what the Pastor had shared. So, over the next thirty days I continued doing the Mirror Exercise and everyday it got easier and easier until eventually the words I was affirming to myself felt more like my truth.

I cannot say that the exercise was easy, nor that it cured me of ever having to utilize affirmations ever again. In fact, today I teach my clients how to do the Mirror Exercise and I decided to write an *Affirmation Workbook* (available on **Amazon**).

I appreciate that affirmations are a powerful tool, but what made the exercise so much more enriching was looking into the mirror into my own eyes. I realize that it is easy for us to repeat a series of words or phrases to ourselves with no feeling or connection to those words. However, it is hard to say those words while looking into deep into your own eyes. It is impossible for you to lie to yourself. In that respect "the mirror does not lie." It truly does reflect back whatever truth we hold deep inside.

Stop Blaming Others'; Pick Up A Mirror

Not long ago I met a woman named Emily. I met her while living next door to her in South Carolina. Emily was married to a guy named George and while they seemed like a nice enough couple there was something about Emily that was very sad.

During the time I lived next door to Emily and George I was in a relationship with James who was a Staff Sargent in the United States Army. The relationship I was in was pretty serious, as James asked me to marry him. However, I was still on the fence about marrying James considering he displayed some red flags that made me feel uncomfortable.

Nonetheless, we lived together briefly next door to Emily and George who we would connect with periodically. However, the connection between us was more neighborly than friendly.

One night James and I heard Emily and George arguing something fierce and while James was not eager to butt his nose into other people's business, I was concerned the arguing might lead to domestic violence. George's voice was pretty loud and raised while Emily was crying and pleading with him not to leave her. The experience reminded me of the abusive relationship I had previously been in, however no one ever came to see if I needed help or if I was okay.

I decided to knock on Emily and George's door, not knowing how things might play out. George opened the door, smiling, flailing his arms up and inviting me in to speak with Emily.

"Would you please tell her that I am not cheating on her?" He stated. "I think she's so upset because she's pregnant and her hormones are going crazy. I just want to run to the store," he said. "Please talk to her."

Once I was involved in George and Emily's situation, I realized I did not really want to be. My objective was to make sure Emily was okay and to politely let them know to quiet down their argument. I had no intention to enter their apartment and speak to Emily about what was going on in her relationship. To this day, I have many regrets about getting involved and I will tell you why:

George invited me into their place so that I could "Talk some sense" to Emily. "I'll leave you two alone to talk. I'm going to go have a beer."

"No, please don't go," Emily cried.

"I'm not going nowhere. I'll be right out front or walk next door to ole boy's spot if that's alright with him," George argued.

Apparently, James was "old boy" and the porch was the front steps of the apartment duplex we shared with them.

Once George was gone I asked Emily to share what was upsetting her.

"I'm five months pregnant and instead of coming straight home from work he stays out late with some friends from work. I am really sick all the time and can barely cook anything for myself, let alone keep it down ifI do. I need him home to help me, but he acts as if he doesn't want to be around me. To be honest, I think he's cheating on me. I can just feel it."

Considering Emily and I never had too much to say to one another aside from the casual salutations about the weather I felt like she had shared more than I had expected. I did not really have an answer for her considering I did not know George very well. However, I decided to say something that would ease her mind.

"Perhaps George is right, that you're feeling a bit overwhelmed because of your hormones. He appears to love you from what I've seen. And, it's somewhat common for men to draw closer or pull back during a woman's pregnancy."

"Really?" She asked.

"Trust me, I know. I have four kids and from what I've seen men behave strangely around their pregnant wives. Perhaps you should give him some space," I suggested. "Allow him to get a grip on the fact that he's going to become a father, which he may be feeling is a huge responsibility and perhaps that it will infringe on what little free time he has. I will be right next door, so if you need something to eat, I will be happy to help you until he gets home. How does that sound?"

"Thank you," She replied. "I would appreciate that. Maybe you're right. Maybe I'm just trippin."

"Yes, maybe you just need to chill and relax and try to stay calm and happy for your baby."

Emily and I talked a bit longer while I warmed her up a can of soup and gave her some crackers to go along with it. By the time I said goodnight she was smiling and a lot calmer than she was prior to my knock on the door. I wish I could say I felt good for cheering her up.

I did not. Because, a part of me wondered if her reservations about George was true, that in fact he was cheating.

Nonetheless, there was nothing I could do about it, nor could she. And, her being upset would do no good to her baby. I decided it was best not to share my suspicions with Emily and to have as little involvement as possible. Unfortunately, that did not happen.

I wish I could say that things between Emily and George improved after our talk. But, things only got worse. George continued to stay out late. In fact, one night he did not bother to go home. I know this because about 2 a.m. one morning Emily knocked on our door crying because George was not home. She wanted to know if she could call him from one of our mobile phones, or the house phone. We invited her in so she could make her call.

After several attempts to reach George by our house phone Emily got no response, which understandably made her even more distressed. In fact, she was so upset that she asked if either of us would drive her around town to look for him.

"Emily," I said, "I do not think that's a good idea. It's pretty late and it's not a good idea for any of us to be driving around at this hour. Let alone you, being seven months pregnant and all. I think it's best you try to get some rest and if you haven't heard from George by the morning one of us will drive you around to have a look."

Reluctantly, Emily agreed and I walked her back to her apartment. She once again confessed that she believed George was cheating.

"I'm certain of it," she said.

I chose not respond. Yet, that night I had a hard time sleeping because I felt torn between doing what I felt was right and minding my own business. As chance would have it, I ended up choosing to do the right thing. However, this decision did not end well for me.

A few weeks had passed since George stayed out all night. And, while things had not improved between the two of them, things did not appear to be worse. One evening George came knocking on our door for James. Seemingly, he was hoping James would drive him to the store to pick up a six pack of beer. Emily was visiting a friend of hers on the other side of town and since they only had one car he did not have a ride of his own.

James agreed to drive him to the store and not because he actually liked George, but because I begged him to get the scoop on what was really going on. At the time I thought it was a good idea and gave him a list of things to pick up to make the experience seem a bit more legit.

James did not get home from his store run with George for nearly two hours. And, when he returned he had an earful as to why. It seems Emily's suspicions were correct – George was cheating. But, according to him he was trying to break it off with the woman he was cheating with. According to James, this was the real reason George needed a ride, because he wanted James to drive him to his mistress's home so he could call the whole thing off, "once and for all." He figured if he showed up with James, the woman would take him more serious and leave him alone. However, the only way the woman would agree to leave George alone is to have sex with her one last time, which George complied.

"What! Well, where were you while they were having breakup sex?" I asked.

"I was waiting in the car. I had no idea they were having sex until he came back down to the car and told me. I was actually just about to leave his ass, when he came running out with a dumb smile on his face and tidying up his clothes."

"You're kidding!"

"Nope! Wish I was." James said shaking his head. "This guy thinks he's the ultimate player, but he looks more like a fool to me."

I cannot say that I was surprised that George was cheating. Having experienced being cheated on myself I understood very well that gut feeling a woman gets in the pit of her stomach when she suspects her lover is cheating on her.

It was at this moment I made my mind up and decided the next time Emily asked me if I thought George was cheating, or she told me her thoughts, I would confess what I knew. However, I decided I would do it strategically so as to minimize the impact she felt once she found out.

Turns out, Emily would not be as "impacted" by George's cheating as I would.

Emily was nearing her ninth month of pregnancy when she knocked on my door crying one afternoon. She was crying and extremely upset because she found proof that George was cheating and wanted my opinion as to whether she should confront him. Finally! I thought. I was so happy she had proof and that this whole horrible experience would be over. However, once she shared her evidence with me, which was only a series of outgoing calls from his mobile to the same number, I realized she did not have the proof she actually needed. So, I did what I felt I would want any friend to do for me. I told her, but not directly. I found the best way for her to hear the truth.

I invited Emily into my apartment and sat her down. I figured it was best she be sitting when I delivered the bad news. After she was sitting somewhat comfortably, I went into my bedroom, grabbed my mobile and proceeded to call James. I told Emily not to make a sound as I placed the call to James with the speaker on. We both sat silently listening to James's mobile ring.

"Hello," James answered on the other end of the call.

"Hey," I replied. "You got a second?"

"Sure, What's up?"

"Well, Emily came by today. She was really upset."

"Yeah, and what's new?"

"Well, I'm thinking we should tell her about George. I mean I came this close to telling her myself, but would like it if you and I told her together when you get back."

"I really don't think we should get any more involved than we are, but if you really think this will help her, then that's what we gotta do."

"Yes, I think we have to tell her. Anyway, she said she has the woman's phone number," I said.

"Well, she doesn't need the woman's phone number. She works right up there with him where he works. I think he brought her around their place if I'm not mistaken."

"She works with him?"

"Yes! At that nursing home you used to work at. They work in the kitchen or housekeeping or something. Yeah, the woman works with him and if I'm not mistaken he brought her to the house."

"Wow!" I said.

"Well, that's who this guy is. He has little regard for his wife or his baby. Let's sort it out when I get back."

"Okay," I said. "Bye, talk to you later."

Emily sat shivering with tears streaming down her cheeks. I sat down next to her holding her in my arms as she sobbed for what felt like forever. I held her like a baby while she wept in my arms, telling her how beautiful she was and how things would get better.

"You have a beautiful baby boy coming soon and he's going to need you to be strong for him."

"I can't do this by myself," She cried.

"Sure, you can. Women make it on their own every day. You will be fine. Plus, I don't think George is going to leave you on your own. From what I know he was trying to break it off with the woman anyway. So, you're going to be fine. People make it through worse things, Emily."

"How long have you known and why didn't you tell me?"

"Look Emily, I haven't known that long and besides George was trying to break it off with the woman, so I didn't want to upset you. The only reason I said anything today, which I really didn't say anything. You overheard a conversation between me and James. But, the reason I said something today is because you said you had proof he was cheating."

"Well, thank you for telling me," Emily said as she tried to stand up from the couch. "I'm going to go home, take a nap and figure out what I'm going to do."

"That sounds like a good idea," I said, walking her to the door. "I think you just need to get some rest so you can clear your head. We can chat more when you wake up, okay?"

"That's fine," she said.

I watched Emily walk into her apartment, then went back into my apartment to lay down and take a nap. The whole ordeal was quite draining. Let alone, it brought up a great deal of emotions and heartache for me. I could relate to her situation because I had been cheated on when I was pregnant with my son. Like Emily, I had a nagging suspicion that my husband at the time was cheating. However, I did not have a good friend like me to tell me, nor hold my hand when the truth came out.

I was awakened by a loud and rapid knock on my apartment door. I looked at the nightstand clock and realized that I had been sleeping for nearly two hours. Groggily, I got up to answer the door to see who it was. James was called away on duty and would be away for two nights so I knew it wasn't him. I opened the door to see Emily fully dressed and pacing.

"What's going on Emily? Did you get some sleep?" I asked.

"Yes. Well, not really." She replied. "Well, what can I do for you?" I asked. "Will you drive me to George's job?"

"What! Why?" I asked confused.

"I called him and confronted him over the phone. He asked me to come up to his job so we can talk."

"Emily, I really think you should wait until he comes home. Perhaps now is not the right time for you to go up to his work place. You're due any day now. Why don't you wait for him to get home to discuss this?"

"Well, I thought about waiting, but then I realized he might not come home. He might just leave me, or go to her house or something. No! I wanna go up to his job now. Will you take me?" She pleaded.

"Okay Emily, let me get my things. I'll be right with you."

"Thank you! I'll wait for you by the car."

I had a bad feeling about driving Emily to George's work. But, at the time I did not feel like I had a choice. Somehow, I had convinced myself that I had to see the whole ordeal through to the end, if not for Emily, then for me.

George worked at a long-term nursing home I had worked at when I was an LPN (Licensed Practicing Nurse). I wound up quitting that gig to go work at a hospital that offered to more pay per hour. I am not sure this particular facility ever got over it. Nevertheless, I knew exactly where we were going.

Neither Emily, or I said a thing the entire drive up, which for me, made the drive almost unbearable. In hindsight, I wish Emily and I had talked or made a plan prior to our arrival. Unfortunately, we did not and this would be a mistake I lived to regret.

Once we arrived at the facility Emily got out of the car and proceeded to the back entrance near the kitchen, which is where George worked. Since we did not speak about a plan and did not talk on the way up, I was not too sure if I should wait or leave her with George. I decided to wait at least ten minutes, I told myself. However, five minutes had not even gone by before Emily returned.

"Wow! That was quick," I said.

"We're not done talking yet. He wants to talk to you."

"To me? Hmm, why does he want to talk to me?" I asked.

"Because I told him what you told me."

"What I told you? Wait a minute, I didn't tell you anything. I let you listen to a conversation between me and James," I replied.

"Yeah, well that's what I told him and he asked if he could talk with you?"

Everything in me was telling me to get in my car and drive away. To leave them to sort out their own mess. To not get any more involved. But, I did not listen to that voice and instead, I locked up the car and followed Emily over to where George was. After all, I thought, what's the worst that can happen? I'm on public property. They have cameras and this is his job. What's he going to do? Well, here's what happened:

Emily and I walked into the kitchen entrance of the nursing facility. However, when we arrived George was not alone. He was standing alongside two other women. Two women I had never seen before. I walked in uneasily not knowing what to expect. Until a dark skinned tall Black woman approached me, yelling at me and asking me why I had lied on her.

"Excuse me?" I replied, confused because I had no idea who this woman was. I assumed from her body language and tone of voice that this was the mistress. However, since there were two women other than me and Emily standing there, I was not sure.

"You heard me. You're a lying ass Bitch!" she yelled.

At that point, I looked at George and then to Emily and said, "Emily, I don't have time for this. I don't know what this is about. You know what you heard and you know I don't have any reason to ruin your relationship. I'm not going to stand for this."

"You're lying because you're a sneaky jealous Bitch. And, I'm going to whip your ass for lying on me and this man."

By this point, I had no intention of trying to explain myself, nor to continue the conversation with this woman. So, I turned to let myself out of the kitchen, when suddenly I was grabbed by the back of my hair and dragged down to the floor by this crazy woman. She was dragging me by my hair, ripping hair follicles as she pulled. Although I was in a lot of pain I managed to grab her by the ankle so that she tripped and was now on the floor face-to-face with me. Yet, somehow she wound up on top and began sitting on my chest and smashing my head against the hard cold floor.

I felt myself slipping into silence as this crazy woman slammed my head against the dirty concrete kitchen floor. When all of a sudden, I was brought back into consciousness by someone's foot kicking me in my side. I managed to look to see who it was — it was the short dark-skinned woman that was standing next to the woman on top of me when I first came into the kitchen space.

I knew I had to do something and at least make an attempt to fight one of these women back, or I was going to die. So with everything in me, I reached my hands up to the woman's face that was sitting on top of me and proceeded to gouge her eyeballs out. I dug my fingers into her sockets so deeply I thought I was going to pull her eyeballs out.

"My eye!!" She screamed. "My eyes! Stupid Bitch tried to pull out my eyes!"

Fortunately, for her, she still did have her eyes. But, I was not sure how fortunate I would be if I did not get up and run to my car, which is exactly what I did.

With my head pounding, black eyes and blood pouring down the side of my head, I managed to make it to my car door, only turning back once to make sure no one was behind me.

Once I unlocked the door, I searched for my first aid kit so I could clean my face off enough to drive myself home, or to a hospital. As I was feeling my way around under the back seat of the passenger side for the first aid kit, I hear a knock on my window. It was Emily and George. I spoke to them through the closed window still searching for the kit, but not taking my eyes off of them.

"What do you want?"

"Would you give us a ride home? George can drive seeing you're in no condition to drive like that," Emily said.

"Right," I responded. "No thanks to you."

"I did not know they were going to do that," She replied.

"Whatever! I really don't want to hear this, nor do I have time for this."

"Collette, please open the door. You cannot drive home like that. Come on, let us help," George chimed in.

"You know George, I would never be in this mess if you were man enough to ... You know what, you're not even worth it. Neither of you. Now get away from my car before I call the police. And, find your own way home. Don't worry about me. I'm going to be fine."

I decided it was better that I not waste any more time on the property and thought that perhaps someone might call the police, which could make me look like the trespasser. So, I started my car up and drove home, bloodied and all.

By the time I reached my apartment, I was quite frightened by what my neighbors might try to do to me. So, I dragged large pieces of furniture to block the front door, took a shower and some Ibuprofen, and went to bed. I wound up having to call out of work for the next two days because my eyes were swollen and sealed shut. I definitely had much better days than this one.

By the time James got back home from being in the field he was quite angry over what I shared over the phone. I did not know just how angry he was until he arrived. As he walked into the house, he kissed me on my forehead, which was the only part of my face not swollen and bruised and then he proceeded to the closet in the bedroom and pulled out a small box. He then walked over to the dresser and pulls out another box, and grabbed a key. He then pulls out the box contents; a gun. He quickly loads it with bullets, then tells me to get dressed and to follow him.

"James, please tell me what is going on. What are you going to do?"

"Don't say anything, just get your clothes on and follow me. Now!"

Shaking, I got dressed and followed James out the front door and straight to the neighbor's apartment. He knocked and waited. Emily opened the door.

"Yes?" she said, bewildered.

"Where's your husband?" James asked coldly.

"George! James is at the door here looking for you."

George comes to the door trying to act cheery. "What's up, Man?"

"You see this woman right here?" James said pointing to me.

"Yeah Man, I'm real sorry about that," George said trying to sound apologetic.

At this point James pulls the gun out of his pocket. Later, I would learn that it was a .45 automatic pistol, but at the time it just looked like a big, black, heavy gun. When George saw the gun he raised his hands up in the air and began pleading and begging.

"Alright, alright now, listen Man! You don't need to do this. Don't do nothing crazy."

We all stood silent, with no one saying a word. Time seemed to stand still. What was probably less than a minute felt like an eternity. Then, finally James said in a voice I had never heard:

"Don't you ever put your hands on her ever again, do you hear me?" James said to George.

"I didn't put my hands on her," George pleaded.

"And, you're lucky you didn't because if you did, you'd be dead right now," James said. "From now on you don't know us. Don't either of you knock on our door and don't you dare say anything to her, do you hear me? Matter of fact, when you see her, walk the other way, or wait until she doesn't have to see you. Do you hear me?"

"Yes, I got you man. I'm sorry!" George replied. "I got you loud and clear. I'm really sorry."

"Good, I hope you do hear me. Because if I ever go away and have to hear anything like this happens to her again, or you or that witch in there speak to her or anything, I'm going to put a bullet in your head. Got me?"

"Yes!" George replied.

A few days later Emily gave birth to a healthy baby boy and a week or so later, she and George moved out. They never spoke to me again and I never said anything to either of them.

I guess you might be thinking that I was upset and felt betrayed by Emily and George. Quite to the contrary. As I think back to those times, I realize that most of what I felt for Emily was compassion that I wish someone had for me when I was being cheated on. I also appreciated that I had no one else to blame but myself. Because, I came to understand that it was not Emily I was really seeking justice for; it was for myself.

When my ex-husband cheated on me there were no friends, or good neighbors to come to my rescue. My instincts told me my ex was cheating and there were even signs. However, I did not trust my own voice, nor my own instincts to do anything about it. In fact, even after I learned of my ex-husband's extramarital affair I did not confront him, I attacked the woman he was having the affair with. Instead, I tried to salvage the relationship I had with the man who betrayed me, which is why Emily's story resonated with me so deeply.

I somehow convinced myself that if I could save Emily from her circumstances, that somehow I could save myself. I am not saying that I deserved to be attached and beaten up by two savage women. However, blaming Emily for the choices I made was not fair either.

I asked myself whether I would make the same choice to tell a friend that her partner was cheating on her, and the answer is, yes! Because, many women and men that have been the victim of cheating have this desire to do the right thing and make right the wrongs for others that have gone through their same experience. The thing people that have been cheated on do not realize (and it took me some time to learn this) is that cheaters cheat because they have a low self-esteem and often, the cheating has nothing to do with the person being cheated on.

Sure, the person being cheated on gets hurt and has to deal with the pain and rejection. Still, the cheater lives a life as a cheater and a liar because that is who they are and perhaps, will always be. Perhaps both the cheater and the one cheated on are mirror images of one another and can only change the experiences they both have when they are brave and capable enough of looking in the mirror and loving themselves.

CHAPTER SIX

Magic Frogs

"No Dancing Mice – No Singing Teapots."

At the beginning of the book I talked about having been married more times than I cared to share. Well, to be exact, I have been married four times and that includes the current marriage I am in now. You might be asking yourself, "Who am I to give dating and relationship advice about love?" Or, "Why should you be listening to me, or reading my book for that matter?" And, the answer is quite simple; because I am just like you because no one's relationships are, or ever have been, perfect.

My hope is that as you continue reading these stories, you find your story and solve your dating and relationship challenges. In the meantime, just know that that you are not alone. We are not alone.

Kissing Lots Of Frogs

I am sure you heard of the phrase that you have to "kiss a lot of frogs" to get your Prince. However, what exactly does that mean?

As little girls our parents tell us, "One day you will meet the one." Disney teaches us that, "One day we will live happily ever after." However, no one ever tells us just how many frogs we will have to kiss, date, have sex with and perhaps marry, until we find the right one.

It took me a long time to "find my happily," and though today I am happily married to my best friend and soulmate, I used to believe that I needed to kiss a lot of frogs to find my Prince. That is, until one day I realized the only thing you will get kissing a lot of frogs is warts.

Perhaps all of what we have been told about kissing frogs is bogus — simply not true. Sure, we may have to date a lot of partners to find our perfect partner. However, when we learn to be loving, happy human beings and grateful for all that we have, we are likely to attract truly viable suitors, rather than sifting through a swamp full of frogs.

Prior to fully appreciating that I needed to love myself before I was capable of being in a loving committed relationship with someone that loved me and whom I loved, I kissed a lot of frogs. Yep, I was deep down in the swamp. I was living under the assumption that finding my perfect partner was a numbers game and I was willing to reach the top score in order to find my true love.

What I did not see, nor comprehend at the time is the reason I dated and married so many unsuitable prospects before meeting my ideal partner was because I had no idea who I was, nor what I really wanted. It is as though I was fishing (with all the right gear), but I did not know exactly what kind of fish I was fishing for. Only that I wanted to eat fish, because I thought fish would be good for me, not really understanding why.

Most self-help books and dating experts will tell you that finding the right relationship is a numbers game. Perhaps there is some degree of truth to that. However, I like to think of finding the one terms like this:

Let us look at money as an example. I read somewhere that people in a bank do not learn how to identify counterfeit bills. Instead, they learn how to identify real money. They learn the color of real money, the print, the smell, the feel, the coding and many other details. They study what real money looks like, day in and day out, so that in the event they run across a counterfeit bill, they know that it is fake. Why? Because they studied real money.

Finding our perfect partner should be no different than learning how to spot a fake hundred-dollar bill. Hence, if we learn what a loving, meaningful relationship looks like we can spot a fake when we see it.

Thus, we will not end up having to "kiss a lot of frogs" hoping to find a Prince.

A Frog Prince?

Who in their right mind would choose to kiss a slimy warty frog? Ugh! However, we are prompted over and over again, that in order to find our Prince Charming, we have to kiss a lot of frogs.

Once again, I blame fairy tales for filling our heads with the harmful notion that frogs eventually become Princes. In Grimm's fairy tale *The Frog Prince*, we learn about a young Princess that made a promise to befriend a frog in exchange for finding her favorite ball. Unbeknownst to the Princess, the frog was a handsome young Prince trapped under some sort of spell.

However, for one reason or another (and there is no valid reason for kissing a reptile in my opinion) she kissed the frog and *voila*, she broke the spell revealing that her frog friend was actually disguised as a handsome Prince.

In my opinion, *The Frog Prince* may be the most harmful fairy tale. It leads little girls to live under the notion that you can turn something slimy into something meaningful, rather than focusing on the actual qualities a person possess. Sure, some people can change and some bad boys do become good guys. But, is it our job to change the people we are with? We either accept them for who they are, or we set ourselves up for failure

I will admit, that since I have had my fair share of marriages and committed relationships I cannot tell you that you should ditch this belief. Hell, at one time or another I adopted the creed, "if at first you don't succeed, try, try again." Thankfully, I threw that ridiculous idiom out the window also.

Nevertheless, living under the principles that others told me did not help my cause, which explains why I went through a series of really bad relationships before I met and married the husband I married to today. In fact, it was not until I "found my happily," that I was at peace with myself and began intentionally dating that I was able to attract the man I am with today.

CHAPTER SEVEN

No Rules, No Pretending

Life Can Be Challenging; Dating & Relationships Do not Have to Be

When I began my journey to learn why so many self-help books unintentionally gave such false and harmful advice when it came to matters of the heart, or to understand why self-help books worked for some, but did not work for others, I learned a couple of things.

The first thing I discovered when reading self-help books (particularly, those filled with "how-to" instructions) is that it is we who decide whether to do what we are instructed to do (or not).

By the same token, if the instructions we are given are unrealistic, unattainable, or retain a more cookie-cutter format that does not connect with our core values or beliefs, then we are likely to reject what we are being told to do.

People purchase self-help guides with the intentions of changing something they have a hard time changing about themselves; to learn something they do not know, and/or to validate a belief they already have about something. Therefore, whether a self-help book works is solely dependent on the reader. However, this does not take away the fact that many of the self-help books on the market, particularly those that concerns matters of the heart, are simply no good. Let's have a look at some of the books I read, and I will show you what I mean.

Shove Your Rules Where The Sun Don't Shine

The first self-help book I ever read was called *The Rules,* by Ellen Fein and Sherrie Schneider. *The Rules,* which was published in the Nineties, instructed women to throw out everything they thought they knew about love and relationships (including their self-worth and self-respect) in exchange for winning the heart of "Mr. Right."

The Nineties woman was not as free and liberated as some of the women in the Sixties, but she was free and empowered (and somewhat equal to men). She was the

CEO of her own firm, owned property, had a variety of birth-control to choose from and she was free to vote and have meaningless sex. However, *The Rules*, was anything but empowering. In fact, *The Rules* was all about teaching women how to control their natural urges to be themselves, while pretending to be someone they were not in order to snag a man.

What these "Evil Queens" failed to include in their evil master plan, is how to live "happily ever after" once you and your Prince moved into his magnificent castle and he found out you were: Not put together, nor mysterious, incompatible, desperate, needy, that your feet are too big, you have fibroids, have children, you are a divorcee, have arthritis, do not enjoy cooking, were a battered wife and have a desire to save the world because you so desperately want to learn how to save yourself.

The theme throughout their entire book was to pretend as if you had no desire to be loved, even if that was what you so desperately yearned for. Of course, most women failed to measure up as a "Creature Unlike Any Other": A woman that denied yearning for sex or companionship, wore fashionable, sexy clothes (even though she preferred Cuddle Duds or comfy sweats), never laughed loud or told jokes and always wore makeup (even if she had bad skin). "Rules Girls," got nose jobs, grew their hair long, wore short skirts with sheer pantyhose and never, ever asked a guy out on a first, second or third date.

The Rules promised women that became "Rules Girls" would: Never have anxiety, or have to worry about saying the wrong thing, never be physically abused, because the man of your dreams would treat you like a delicate flower, never be cheated on, need counseling, or have to suffer a messy divorce. However, as it turns out in 2011 Ms. Fein was reportedly getting a divorce, which either means she was not truly a "Rules Girl," or she stopped living by her own rules.

In addition to instructing women on how to behave, i.e., how to pretend in order to catch a man, Fein and Schneider also told women how men thought, and what men really wanted such as: He never gets angry, loves your idiosyncrasies, gets angry when you ignore him, desires you do everything with him, never gets bored of you, loves for you to call him at work, loves to watch you and listen to you talk and he whistles at you when you walk around the house scantily clothed.

The Rules convinced unmarried women that by doing The Rules, they would meet and marry the man of their dreams and live happily ever after together forever. It persuaded married women to turn their marriage into a Rules marriage if they were not getting what they wanted within their marriage.

Prior to my happy, loving marriage (which by the way, I did not get into following *The Rules*) I tried desperately to become a Rules Girl. And, when I failed, I blamed myself for not being good enough, or as *The Rules* referred to, "A Creature Unlike Any Other."

Instead, I was simply me and unable to pretend to be someone else. Instead, I called my future husband first and asked him out on our first date. We had sex before we were married and (in spite of what *The Rules* said) I laughed out loud, rarely wore sheer stockings prior to our marriage and told goofy slapstick jokes.

No, I was not a Rules Girl, nor would I ever be. However, it took me reading poor books like *The Rules*, to let me know that in reality, all I had to do to snag the heart of Mr. Right was love myself, wholly and completely.

Comedians Don't Have All The Answers

After reading The Rules, I read several other books on the market such as: *Why Men Love Bitches* (they don't! In fact, nobody does), *Have Him At Hello* (he will keep on walking, since that's what people do when you greet them, but they don't know you), and *How to Catch and Keep A Man*, (which was downright problematic and terrible advice). And, just when I thought the dating books could not get any worse, two more books (written by comedians) hit the market – (note to self; if a person tells jokes for a living, perhaps they are not the best person to take dating or relationship advice from).

Act Like A Lady, Think Like A Man, written by Steve Harvey, and *He's Just Not That Into You*, written by Greg Behrendt and Liz Tuccillo. Both books claim to want to help women get treated better by men. Harvey's claims that the objective in his book is to empower women by providing them with a wide-open view into the minds of men. While, Behrendt and Tuccillo's book aims to teach women how to identify men that are not interested in dating for the long haul.

Both books have been successfully adapted into movies. However, each fails miserably at offering up any useful or sound advice that can genuinely help women create and sustain meaningful romantic relationships and here's why:

As I mentioned early on, there are no cookie-cutter formats when it comes to matters of the heart. However, each book suggests that there is a general standard way that men think, while implying at the same time, that all women want the same things when it comes to relationships.

Upon reading both of these books (at first out of curiosity, then for research for this book) it appears as if each author portrayed men as barbaric creatures that think with the "head with the vein" over the "head with the brain." While, at the same time signifying that if women are to control both heads, they would need to deceive men.

Gender narratives like these complicate relationships because they lead men to believe they are not good enough to be with a woman, therefore feeling immense pressure to impress women, to perform for them, to show off their money, or their station in life. These behaviors reinforce feelings of worthlessness as well as sexual anxiety. Men are then led to believe that if they do not exclaim their love for a woman, even when it is too soon, she will not like him.

Similar to men, the gender narrative that women are being subjected to screws up her view of her role in relationships. For instance, women are told to spend their entire lives waiting for a man to do something amazing to impress her, or she is taught how to be compliant and knowledgeable in how men's brains think and work.

Consequently, the approach to finding love that women are forced to take is either the one that spends her entire life waiting for her knight in shining armor to rescue her, because after all she is the prize. Or, she needs to understand Sigmund Fucking Freud's Oedipus Complex, which basically states that as women we are likely to hate our mother's and want to subconsciously marry our fathers.

Like most dating self-help books, *Act Like a Lady, Think Like a Man*, and *He's Just Not That Into You*, are substantiated through perpetuating stereotypes that make assumptions about what women and men think when it comes to love and relationships. However, since most self-help books are aimed at women (who tend to be the bulk of the consumers for books like these), women are made to feel responsible for the success, or the lack of success that she has in her romantic life.

Stop Pretending

Life Can Be Challenging;
Dating and Relationships Don't Have to Be.

When we are led to believe that our relationship has to be picture-perfect based off of the media's standards, we have a hard time creating our own standard of happiness. Take for instance:

In the media the path that leads to "happily ever after" begins with fireworks, which leads to passionate sex, which creates a false sense of connection, that generates little to no conflict, which ends in a false sense of belonging. It is the same age old formula: girl meets boy, girl obsesses over boy, boy disappoints girl, then girl does something stupid to make boy chase her.

Finding your perfect partner is just the beginning. Learning to check your emotional baggage and being willing to compromise and communicate in healthy ways are all part of the journey.

However, in order to create and sustain a meaningful romantic relationship we must first be healthy and happy on our own two feet. That way, we are capable and ready to attract a healthy and happy partner. Ultimately, our version of "happily ever after" will be uniquely our own. In my opinion, that is much better than any fairy tale you will ever read about!

CHAPTER EIGHT

Finding Happily...

Happily Ever After Is Not An Ending;
It's a Journey

As women, soon as we are old enough we are bombarded with fairy tale images and stories of how wonderful our lives will be as soon as we become a wife and a mother. While fairy tales do have a place in our society -- in magical stories set in imaginary places – life is not pulled straight out of a storybook and true love does not begin with the first kiss or even the first date; it begins and ends with SELF .

Perhaps, if we want to attract more love into our lives or if our desire is to truly be happy, then begin and end with a healthy love of SELF. We have nothing to prove to other people, because what matters is simply that we approve of ourselves. And we can, fully and without pretending. We can love ourselves knowing that we are loved deeply by God and that we have a real purpose for being born and living. We can love ourselves no matter our faults, because every one of us is on a journey to live, learn and love.

What I learned in writing this book is that fairy tales, (whether they are the ones from our childhood, or the romantic comedies we come to enjoy as adults) involve unrealistic views about love and life, leading many of us to believe that the Prince of our dreams will end up being our lifelong partners if we compromise ourselves for the sake of living "happily ever after." Our reality is frequently far different. A vast number of us wind up settling for a life partner who, although not perfect, is "perfect enough for us," even though the love we share isn't lifted straight out of the pages of a fairy tale.

You might be asking, "Collette now that I have read this book, and *if* this is the last dating and relationship book I will ever need, what do I do now? How am I to find love?"

At the risk of sounding too simplistic, true love begins and ends with SELF. Therefore, I recommend your foundation begins with the following suggestions.

Where to Go From Here?

Forgiveness

Forgiveness is a powerful tool, one that I used to release and let go of my old stories about love and relationships, as well as a tool I use daily to allow for the space to let love in. Forgiveness is not about letting someone that has wronged you off the hook, or giving someone a pass to walk all over you. It is about having the freedom to live life fully on your own terms.

Often, our inability to find love, or attract our perfect partner coincides with some past trauma or pain we experienced from someone we loved. However, by holding onto the experience we block our ability to open ourselves up to receive the love we say we want. In this respect we should do the "Forgiveness Process."

The Forgiveness Process is an exercise that helps us learn how to forgive ourselves and others so that we can attract the love we deserve. There are many books on the market that will show you how to forgive, however if you are looking for a short easy guide to get you started, you can order a book I published on **Amazon** called, *The Forgiveness Process Workbook*. Check out the recommended readings in the next chapter to learn more.

Gratitude

Gratitude is another powerful tool that helps to bring about more love into our lives. People that are grateful for what they have attract more reasons to be grateful.

When we are not getting the love we want it is hard to find reasons to be grateful. We see other people being happy and doing things with their significant others and we want those things for ourselves.

Instead of yearning for what you do not have, or for not having an experience you want, focus on what you do have and find things in your life to be grateful for. Most people understand the concept of being grateful. We experience moments of gratitude when something we hoped for works out in our favor. However, many people find it hard to be in a general state of gratitude, particularly when things are not working out.

The key is to exercise a state of gratitude all the time without a particular reason, or situation. Sure, things will happen that make you sad and there will be reasons or days you just do not feel good. However, people that exercise gratitude in the most challenging times tend to attract more favorable experiences into their lives.

FINDING HAPPILY · 167

There are many books on the market that will show you how to forgive, however if you are looking for a short easy guide to get you started, you can order a book I published on **Amazon** called, *The Gratitude Process Workbook.* Check out the recommended resources in the next chapter to learn more.

Meditation & Spiritual Practice

A daily spiritual practice of meditation, affirmations and/or prayer is another tool I highly suggest. Through meditation we get to create a clean slate for the day and reflect on the day we had. Through prayer, or affirmations we get to "thank about what we pray about," as well as call into being what we aim to intend for ourselves.

Meditation, prayer and affirmations can work for you even if you are not a religious or spiritual person. There are guided meditations that help you visualize the life you want and meditations that help you relax, release stress, depression and anxiety. And, affirmations exercises that help you change up your internal dialogue that might not be aligned with what you want in a partner.

There are many health benefits to all three of these modalities, however to get started check out some of the recommended resources I suggest, such apps, websites or links to PDF's.

Years ago people used to view mediation, prayer and affirmations as things "hippy dippy" people did. However, more clinical studies reveal that utilizing these skill sets not only make people appear more attractive, but also helps you to get clear about what you want (and feel good in the process).

A Marriage Contract

Do you want to get married to someone that loves you and who you love back? If you answered yes, then my suggestion is to create a marriage contract with yourself.

Most of us construe marriage as a binding contract and we hold ourselves accountable to that contract. We do not take it lightly. In the eyes of the law a marriage contract is so binding it requires us to seek legal counsel to undo the agreement we signed. This is how serious a contract is.

Therefore, my next recommendation is to write a marriage contract to yourself, agreeing by law and under GOD, what you promise to do "till death do you part." So, often we find it easy to agree to be someone for someone else and we ask that someone be this way for us. However, in order to attract your ideal partner, make this agreement first with yourself.

In this manner, if you agree to love yourself wholly and completely, to be faithful and to cherish the love you have with yourself, then what would that look like?

Prior to my last and most recent marriage, I did not take the previous vows I made as seriously as I could have, had I known the value of loving myself wholly and completely. I said the words and I stood before GOD, however, the words that I spoke were empty and meaningless. In many ways, I did not believe the person standing beside me truly loved me, because at the time I did not fully understand what it meant to love myself.

Before you start dating again, try dating yourself first, then court yourself, then write a contract to marry yourself and standing in front of a mirror, say your vows out loud to yourself. Lastly, honor, cherish and live up to those vows.

I am not recommending this as a "how-to" tool, but because I did it (and, it helped me) I now recommend my clients do it. The idea is that once you are fully ready to love and commit to yourself, you will be ready for your perfect partner to love and commit to you.

Doing What You Love

One of the things single women do whilst waiting for Prince Charming is stop doing the things they love. Instead, they make a list of to-do's that include things they will do once they are living "happily ever after."

However, if you are sitting home alone, doing "the Rules," and waiting for Prince Charming to call before you do something you enjoy, you are missing out on life!

Instead of waiting around, write the following down: Like attracts like! In other words, happy loving people enjoy being around happy loving people. So, start doing the things that make you happy.

Put Yourself Out There

While you are out there doing the things you love, really put yourself out there! This ties into the previous suggestion.

Some of you might already be out there doing the things you love, such as traveling, attending meetups, going to the gym, biking, hiking or attending a book club. However, how many of you are looking to meet your perfect partner doing what you love to do?

So often, we become preoccupied with doing a thing as if it is a chore we mark off our to-do-list. However, what happens when we do this is that we miss out on an opportunity to connect with someone amazing.

On the other hand, if you are not putting yourself out there and if you do not have a hobby, or are not doing something that would make you happy or improve the quality of your life, you are missing the chance to meet someone great.

Keep An Open Heart & An Open Mind

My last and final suggestion is to keep an open heart and an open mind. Staying optimistic is not always easy, particularly when you want to be in a relationship, but just are not having any luck. However, the key is to be thankful and grateful for the blessings you have, and here's why:

Life is going to go on whether you are in a happy meaningful relationship, or not. Since happier people are considered more attractive to everyone around them and they make a more positive impression wherever they go as well, why not choose to do the things that make you happy?

Many people understand the Law of Attraction, however they fail to understand how to apply it, particularly when it comes to matters of the heart. Having an open heart requires the right conditions to let love in. So, in other words if your heart is closed off, you will meet men that are unwilling or incapable of loving you.

One of the things I hear my female friends and clients complain about the most is not being able to attract a man that is "relationship ready." And, they wonder why they keep attracting emotionally unavailable men. What they fail to see is that the men they are attracting into their lives are not necessarily showing up, but responding to the vibrational invitation they are sending out.

CHAPTER NINE

Recommendations & Resources.

Since "Finding Your Happily is not an ending, it is a journey," it is important to connect with the right people, the right places and a *great* community. So that I can help you make that happen, here are my recommendations and resources below:

The Forgiveness Process Workbook will help you release and let go of any stories that are holding you back from finding love and happiness. Through forgiveness we free ourselves and others. Forgiveness is not about letting the other person "off the hook" for wronging you, rather it allows you to release the ties that bind you to the pain they caused. Order your copy of the *Forgiveness Process Workbook* on **Amazon**.

The Gratitude Process Workbook is a book to help you focus on the things in your life to be grateful for. All too often we focus on what we do not want instead of being grateful for the things that bring joy and happiness into our lives. By doing the Gratitude Process you will learn how to be grateful for what you have and thus, attract more things to be grateful for into your life.

Online Dating & Relationship Training Courses are for women and men that are looking to attract quality men or women into their lives and find lasting love. The courses work for singles, divorcee's, and couples looking to improve their relationships. Visit **Teachable Courses** to sign up today: https://find-your-happily-dating-relationship-courses.teachable.com

Follow along with us –
By following @findinghappily on Instagram

Wear one of our Tshirts or Tote Bags –
Part of the proceeds supports victims of domestic violence. Visit https://findinghappily.teemill.com

Join our C&C Book club –
Every month we read fiction and non-fiction books about dating and relationship, personal development, self-help, inspirational and personal empowerment. Join here: https:findinghappily.teemill.com

Are you on our mailing list? Get the latest by joining our mailing list and get FREE dating tips and advice, discounts on our events, products and services, plus stay connected with our online community. Visit: findinghappily.com to sign up.

Travel with us!
Join us for exclusive retreats, workshops and events by visiting: https://findinghappily.com/love-happiness-womens- retreat-hawaii-bahamas/

Other Recommendations

Qigong The Quick & Easy Startup Guide, by Frank Blaney

Ten Percent App

The Answer Is You, by Michael Bernard Beckwith

The Four Agreements, by Don Miguel Ruiz

CHAPTER TEN

F.A.Q.'s.

Is it bad to want to be rescued?

Should we feel guilty if we have the occasional rescue fantasy after being dumped, losing a job, having financial difficulties and seeing all our friends snug in their apparently secure relationships, or more specifically – living happily ever after? The answer is, no! However, waiting for someone to come and rescue you could mean that you are waiting a long time. Instead, start doing what makes you happy and feel good by doing what you *love*. This in turn creates a shift in your energy, because when you are happy and you feel good you become like a magnet attracting the energy you put out right back to you.

What to do if I am in an abusive relationship?

If you think you are in an abusive relationship *there is help*. You can call the National Domestic Violence Hotline to speak with someone about your situation, or call 911 if you need immediate help. Also, you can visit my website at findinghappily.com and submit your question. As a Violence Prevention Specialist I can answer some of your questions about abuse, domestic violence and awareness and connect you to resources.

Should I stop reading self-help books to help me find love?

There are no cookie-cutter formats when it comes to dating and relationships, therefore I do not believe a self-help book can help you find love. On the other hand, there are some helpful self-help books on the market that can give you some useful tools that can help you get clear about what you want and provide ways for you to boost your self-esteem or improve your love life. Still, when it comes to attracting your ideal partner the answer is YOU. And, while you do not have to change who you are or pretend to be someone you are not, you do have to *know* who you are, be clear about what you want, and *be willing* to do what it takes to get it!

Do I have to be perfect to find the man of my dreams?

You do not have to be societies idea of perfection, though you do need to recognize that who you are is already "perfect." The fact that there is no one else like you on this planet — no one that thinks like you, looks like you or feels what you feel. This makes you a unique and perfect being. The question therefore becomes: Should you do anything to improve who you are, the quality of your life and your perception about dating and relationships? The answer is always YES.

You can improve how you think and view the world, thus improving your chances at meeting your perfect partner, or improving your current relationship.

Is there someone out there for everyone?

With 7.6 billion people on the planet, statistically it is very likely that there is someone out there for everyone. The question then becomes: What are you willing to do and how far are you willing to travel to find your perfect partner? Most people will not even travel twenty miles to meet someone new, let alone to an entire new city or continent.

The thing is that most people do not have to travel the entire world to find love. However, the people that would travel the world to find love, will likely find love wherever they go. Why? Because they are open to find love wherever love is.

What happens if I act like myself and no one likes me?

The fact of the matter is that everyone likes different things. However, most people are living under the assumption that they have to pretend to be someone they are not in order for people to like them. The only way you will ever know how people truly feel about you is to start being YOU. The key is to not only be true to yourself, but to fall in love with who you are in the process. People learn to treat us the way they see us treat ourselves. Thus they model the behavior and the tone we set for ourselves. Therefore, if you are loving, kind and compassionate to yourself, you will attract people into your life that are loving, kind and compassionate to you. Sure, other people will show up that do not feel this way about you. However, when you are focused on the qualities you possess, you will see less and less of people that do not share your qualities.

How do I find love?

You do not "find" love — you attract it! Love is something you already possess inside of you. You give it to yourself. You fill yourself with love so that love runs over. You share your love with others and in return you attract people oozing love that want to share their love and their life with you. Therefore, whether you will find love is completely up to you. However, I recommend the first place you look for love is in the mirror and begin and end with YOU.

How can you help me?

As a Dating and Relationship Specialist I help women and men create and sustain meaningful romantic relationships that begin and end with SELF. Therefore, how I help you is to help you release and let go of the story that love is far from you so you can learn to appreciate the beautiful life you have and thus, become a magnet to attract more love into your life. I work with clients 1:1, within groups and/or through my online dating and relationship courses available on Teachable. Keep in mind, I am not a magician. Thus, what you get out of working with me (as well as your success) is completely up to you. Sign up for a Discovery Session today to get started.

ABOUT THE AUTHOR

Collette Gee is the CEO and Founder of **Finding Happily**. **Finding Happily** offers dating and relationship coaching, trainings, workshops and online courses all designed to help women and men succeed in any relationship; be it a romantic, professional, family or platonic.

Collette helps people to create and sustain healthy meaningful relationships that begin and end with SELF. As a Dating & Relationship Specialist, a Certified Violence Prevention Specialist, Certified Neuro-Linguistic Practitioner, and former Psychiatric Nurse Ms. Gee's mission is simple, but profound; to teach people how to love harmoniously and successfully.

Collette currently resides in Los Angeles, California with her husband. She also travels around the world with her team delivering pragmatic dating and relationship trainings that equip participants with life-long tools that help them achieve a healthy balance of their romantic, social, family and professional relationships.

Made in the USA
Las Vegas, NV
25 September 2021